TRINITY COLLEGE

TRINITY COLLEGE

An Historical Sketch

BY

G. M. TREVELYAN, O.M.

MASTER OF THE COLLEGE

1940–51

CAMBRIDGE

TRINITY COLLEGE

1972

First Edition 1943
Reprinted 1943 1946
Reprinted with additions 1972 1976

Printed in Great Britain
at the
University Printing House, Cambridge
(Euan Phillips, University Printer)

CONTENTS

Preface		page vi
Ch. I	Proto-Trinity	1
II	The Early Days of Trinity	13
III	Nevile 1593–1615. The Great Court and the Cloisters	21
IV	How Trinity made the best of Twenty Troublous Years: 1642–1662	34
V	Restoration Trinity. Barrow; Newton; The Library	39
VI	Bentley 1700–1742	51
VII	The Later Eighteenth Century	69
VIII	The New Age; Building of the New Court	88
IX	Trinity in the Victorian Era; Renovation of the Lodge; Growth of Science; Whewell's Court; New Statutes; Cambridge and Trinity; Chapel Decoration	96
X	Montagu Butler 1886–1918	107
Epilogue		114
Index		119

ILLUSTRATIONS

Map of the Site of Trinity before its foundation	page 2
Part of Hammond's map of Cambridge, 1592, just before Nevile's changes	22
The Observatory on the Great Gate From a print 1739–40	55
East Front of the Master's Lodge in 1740 After Bentley's changes, from a print 1739–40	58
Essex's alterations to the Cloisters, 1755–6	70
Trinity College From Loggan's print *circa* 1688	end of book

PREFACE

I have endeavoured to keep errors out of this little book, though doubtless some have crept in. But it has no pretensions to be a work of research, adding to scholarly knowledge. Indeed it has no pretensions at all. I wanted to call it 'The Freshman's Guide to Trinity' but Mr Roberts, of the Press, feared lest that might discourage a wider public. Nevertheless these notes on the buildings and history of the College are meant primarily for Trinity men, old or young, who know as little about Trinity now as I did when I came up in 1893 and, looking round at the Great Court and the Cloisters, wished that someone would tell me something about them.

G. M. TREVELYAN

January 1943

NOTE

I have received valuable help from Sir James Butler and Dr G. Kitson Clark in preparing this edition. A few footnotes have been added, most of them made necessary by changes in the appearance of the College buildings since 1943; these notes are indicated by square brackets. I have also written a new *Epilogue*. Otherwise the text has not been altered.

R. ROBSON

Trinity College
January 1972

A reprint has enabled me to add a few more notes.

R. ROBSON

February 1976.

CHAPTER I

PROTO-TRINITY

GEOGRAPHERS and geologists, for our better instruction, present us with fascinating maps of 'Proto-Britain' or 'Proto-Europe', in which lines indicating the present familiar contours of land and sea are superimposed upon the image of strange and entirely unrecognisable arrangements of earth and water, mountains and rivers: these, we are expected to believe, once occupied the same part of the surface of the terraqueous globe as the very different lands and seas of to-day. Geologic change has transformed that ancient pattern into the modern. The sketch map on p. 2 presents 'Proto-Trinity', making a similar though a smaller demand on the imagination and faith of the reader.

In the fourteenth century there was no College called Trinity. The Great Court did not exist, and the famous area that it has enclosed since the reign of Elizabeth was then traversed by two public thoroughfares, King's Childers Lane running east to west[1] and the end of Mill Street cutting into it from the south. The ground was split up into various small ownerships; orchards, gardens and fields where cattle and horses grazed were divided from one another by green hedges or by ditches full of water, while here and there rose the thatched roof of a house or barn. Farther west, over the future site of Nevile's Court and New Court, water meadows cut by the King's

[1] The King's Childers Lane led down to the landing-place known as Dame Nichol's Hythe, at the south-west end of the present garden of the Master's Lodge. Near here, along the north side of the lane, a substantial private house had been built (afterwards the College Comedy Room—*H* in map, p. 2). Its still remaining south wall is now the south wall of the Master's garden; it has been altered and patched with brick, repaired in many successive centuries, but its stonework is the oldest remaining wall in Trinity.

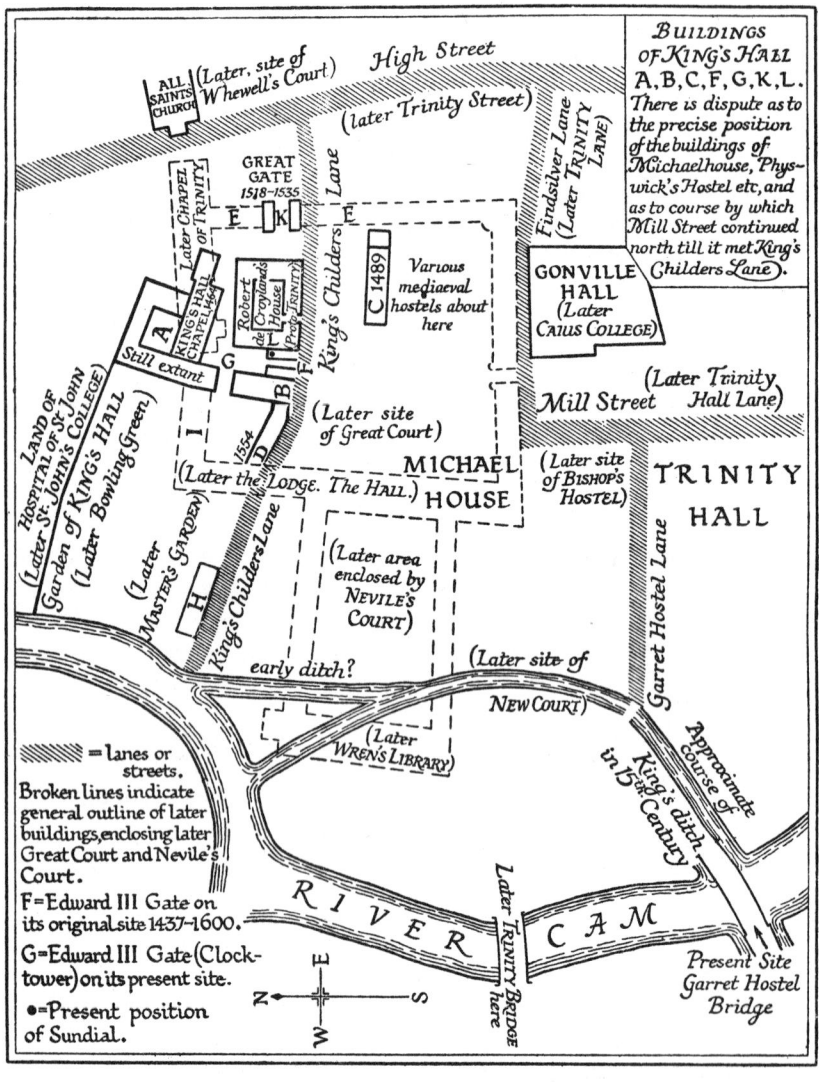

Ditch led down to the landing-places of the river, then the chief commercial highway of Cambridge. (The larger "King's Ditch" was the other side of the town.)

But already in the middle years of the century, at the time of Crecy, Poitiers and the Black Death, there stood a building which we may call 'Proto-Trinity'. Its site is now bare grass and cobbles, between the Chapel, the Great Gate and the sundial. There it rose, amid the fields and orchards, two storeys high, with its walls of wood and its roof of thatch, enclosing a courtyard. This barnlike, rambling old mansion, that has long ago vanished from the sight of men, was the real origin of our College. It had been the private house of Robert de Croyland, but in 1337 Edward III bought it as the permanent home of the Warden and scholars of King's Hall. From that date at latest they lived there, but it is probable that it was the house which Edward II had hired as the residence of their predecessors when he founded King's Hall in 1317.

Sometimes Edward II, sometimes Edward III is called the founder of King's Hall. On the whole Edward II has the better claim, and was regarded as the founder during the Middle Ages, but his more famous and successful son is called 'Fundator Aulae Regis' in the Tudor inscriptions and coats of arms on the outside of the Great Gate, where the unnamed statue of Henry VIII, the undoubted founder of Trinity, standing above the name of Edward III, puzzles the upward gazing tourist.

Following his purchase of the house itself, Edward III bought from various owners several adjoining pieces of land, between the river on the west, the High Street (now Trinity Street) on the east, and St John's Hospital (now St John's College) on the north, so rendering possible the later growth of King's Hall and afterwards of Trinity.

Meanwhile, hard by to the south, another still smaller College was being established. Hervey de Stanton, a lawyer, a Judge and a well-beneficed ecclesiastic, Chancellor of the Exchequer to Edward II, founded Michaelhouse in 1324, seven years after his royal master had founded King's Hall.

De Stanton bought the house of Roger Buttetourte for his purpose. Though nothing of it is left except stones used again by Tudor builders, it may probably claim the honour of having first marked out the lines afterwards adopted for the south-west or Kitchen angle of the Great Court.

And just as Edward III and the early Wardens of King's Hall bought up the small plots of land that lay near their College, so Michaelhouse acquired, by purchase or bequest, other bits of ground, including in 1349 the site of the future south-east corner of Great Court. All these mediaeval patriarchs were not only living their own learned and useful lives, but were unconsciously preparing, by their thrifty acquisitions of new acres, the future spaciousness of Trinity, when Michaelhouse and King's Hall should in fullness of time be made one. But until that union was effected, Gonville Hall (later Caius) and other owners still held portions of the future Great Court area; and several private hostels for non-Collegiate undergraduates occupied various parts of the ground. No prophetic soul was yet dreaming of the things to come.

King's Hall and Michaelhouse were two very different institutions, and each may be said to have contributed an essential part of the character of the College that replaced them.

Michaelhouse was a small society, consisting at first of a Master and half a dozen scholars or Fellows, grown men in Holy Orders; they were persons of humble origin, whose ambitions were limited to the strictly clerical and academic spheres.

King's Hall was a prouder and less rigid seat of learning. It consisted originally of a Warden and some thirty scholars, to whom ere long pensioners were added.[1] So long as the scholars were mere boys (in the first instance they were choirboys from the Chapel Royal sent from Edward II's Court to complete their education), all power and business lay in the hands of their Warden, who was alone responsible to the King

[1] The first pensioner whose admission is recorded is 'William Bardolph, entered on St Vincent's Day, 1387, after dinner'.

for the affairs of the society. But ere long, when the senior scholars were older men such as we should now call Fellows, they gradually drew the management into their own hands, more especially as some of the fifteenth-century Wardens were absent for long periods on important affairs of State—as indeed were other members of the society from time to time.

These scholars and pensioners of King's Hall were many of them sons, relations or protégés of courtiers and civil servants, lay and ecclesiastical. Though not themselves rich, the scholars were well connected and often well born. They aspired to rise high in the service of Church or of State, or of both Church and State together, as was customary in those days when the services rendered to the King were often paid by high promotion in the Church and by benefices held in plurality. A scholar of Michaelhouse, on the other hand, like the ordinary student of the University, would think himself lucky if he ended up in a rural rectory or vicarage. But the scholars of King's Hall were 'the King's childer', after whom the lane that ran by their College was called.

It is believed, though not with certainty, that Chaucer's

> great college
> Men clepe the Soler hall at Cantebrege,

with its 'Wardein' and scholars, is none other than King's Hall. In that case Alein de Strother and his brother scapegrace in the *Reeve's Tale* were 'Proto-Trinity' men. The *Tale* shows that the poet knew Cambridge and its environs well, and a courtier and civil servant like Chaucer would be likely to have acquaintance among the 'King's childer'.

Henry VI gave endowments and privileges to King's Hall, and visited it in person. But it was a dangerous moment when, in 1447, he was so far carried away by zeal for his two new creations, King's College farther down Mill Street, and Eton near his home at Windsor, that he subjected King's Hall to the Provosts of Eton and King's Colleges, who thenceforth were to nominate its Wardens and its scholars. The future Trinity was to be no more than a dumping ground for Etonians!

Fortunately—an Harrovian Master of Trinity may be allowed to think it fortunate—the 'royal saint', having proved 'a sair saint for the Crown', was deposed in 1461. The usurping Edward IV next year restored the independence of King's Hall, or rather made it once more dependent on the Crown instead of on the Provosts of two rival institutions. And therefore when Henry VIII determined to found the greatest of royal Colleges, it was natural for him to enlarge King's Hall, rather than to start wholly afresh on a new site.

Robert de Croyland's timber mansion was soon found too narrow and incommodious for the gentlemen of King's Hall, who were accustomed to such comforts as that simple age could afford. At first additions were made to the original structure: in 1342 a fourth side was added, thereby completely enclosing the courtyard, which had been open on the south. Then in the last years of Edward III's reign (1376–7) a new set of chambers of brick and stone was begun to the north, near the John's boundary. Extensive building operations went slowly on for the next half-century. By 1438 enough new accommodation had been provided to permit of the removal of the venerable but worm-eaten timbers of Robert de Croyland's house: it had served its day, and the earth knew it no more.

The new College buildings included a foursided court (*A* in map, p. 2) of which the west side still exists, the row of brick and stone chambers looking down the Fellows' Bowling Green towards the river. The Bowling Green is the old garden of King's Hall.

There remains also another and more magnificent relic of the fifteenth-century College, the present clock tower or 'Edward III Gateway', so called on account of the late Elizabethan statue of that monarch that decorates its front on the Great Court. This Gateway was completed in 1437, but it did not originally stand where it does to-day. It stood farther forward, where the sundial is now. It was moved back stone by stone to its present position in the year 1600, by the enterprise of Nevile, the 'Master' builder of Trinity, the conceiver and the executant of the idea of the Great Court in its present proportions, with which the Edward III Gateway in its original position interfered. Another line of College chambers (*B* in map, p. 2), afterwards pulled down by Nevile, joined the Gateway in its first position to the Court near the John's boundary.

During the later part of the Wars of the Roses a College Chapel was erected, covering about half the ground now occupied by Trinity Chapel. Before it was built, the scholars of King's Hall had for a century and a half been content to worship in the parish church of All Saints hard by—'All Hallows in the Jewry'. The church itself was pulled down in the nineteenth century, and only its graveyard is left, under the north wall of Whewell's Court. The scholars of Michaelhouse similarly worshipped in St Michael's Church farther down the street, where their founder, Hervey de Stanton, lies buried. Indeed he had rebuilt the church for the uses of his College.

Early in the fifteenth century, King's Hall acquired land on the south side of King's Childers Lane, thereby marching with the Michaelhouse territory. In 1433 leave was obtained by the Warden and scholars to close the eastern part of Childers Lane to the public, and in 1489 a row of College chambers was built on the newly acquired land, parallel to the closed lane but some way back from it on the south (*C* in map, p. 2).

Thus when Henry VIII came to the throne in 1509, the King's Hall buildings, though not forming a complete court, were scattered over a considerable area on both sides of King's Childers Lane. This state of things suggested to the College authorities the idea of erecting a magnificent entrance gateway leading into their grounds from the street; in 1518 and the following years they built the present Great Gate.* Parts of its upper structure and the statues ornamenting its front and back are of later date. But in its essential features the present Great Gate of Trinity stood for some time, in splendid isolation from other buildings, as the final monument of the pride of King's Hall in its latest epoch. It was not built as an entry to our Great Court; on the contrary, the Gate is older than the Court, and helped to dictate its site and proportions.

* [It is now thought that the Great Gate was begun in 1490. *Royal Commission on Historical Monuments. City of Cambridge*, vol. II p. 215. Also true of adjacent buildings.]

Michaelhouse also expanded its buildings after the original occupation of de Buttetourte's house, but its architectural growth was less than that of King's Hall, for it was a poorer and smaller society. None of the buildings of Michaelhouse remain in their original form, though portions may be incorporated in the walls of the Hall, the Kitchens and the Old Combination Room and still more in the chambers of the Great Court that look out at Bishop's Hostel.[1]

From 1497 to 1505 Michaelhouse had for its Master the great and good man John Fisher, to whom John's, Christ's and all Cambridge owe so much It was owing to his influence that the Lady Margaret, mother of Henry VII, in the early years of the sixteenth century, founded St John's College in place of and on the site of the old Hospital of St John (see *John Fisher*, by E. A. Benians, Camb. Univ. Press, 1935).

We have now reached the crisis which transformed King's Hall and Michaelhouse into Trinity, in the last year of Henry VIII. More was at issue than the creation of Trinity, for danger threatened the whole College system which has given Oxford and Cambridge a unique character in the world. But

[1] The author of *Michaelhouse* (privately printed 1924), pp. 57–8, argues with a good deal of force against the views of Willis and Clark in their *Architectural History* (embodied in Fig. 1 for Trinity, No. 23 in their Volume IV, Plans) with regard to the position of 'Le Foule Lane', viz. the northern continuation of Mill Street (later Trinity Hall Lane) across the Michaelhouse grounds to meet Childers Lane. The view of Willis and Clark is that the northern continuation of Mill Street diverged eastward up Findsilver Lane (the present Trinity Lane) and then ran north from the site of the present Queen's Gate of Trinity to the Edward III clock tower, and that the buildings of Michaelhouse extended eastwards as far as the present Queen's Gate. The view of the author of *Michaelhouse* is that Mill Street continued in a straight line northwards, entering the site of the present Great Court near the present Bishop's Hostel Gate, and formed there the eastern boundary of the buildings of Michaelhouse, beyond which, immediately east of Mill Street, lay Physwick's Hostel. Lyne's map of 1574 *pro tanto* supports the view of the author of *Michaelhouse*.

the crisis of 1546 ended by leaving the College system rooted more deeply than ever in the life of England.

In early Tudor times many of the undergraduates of Oxford and Cambridge still lived in private hostels or fended for themselves in the inns and lodgings of the town, subject to little or no discipline. But a considerable proportion were already cared for in Colleges, where they enjoyed comforts and submitted to rules which had been unknown to the ordinary mediaeval students. In 1546 there already existed at Cambridge (in order of foundation) Peterhouse, Clare, Pembroke, Gonville (Caius), Trinity Hall (the College of lay lawyers), Corpus Christi, King's, Queens', St Catharine's, Jesus, Christ's, St John's, and Magdalene. On the other hand the monasteries and friaries attached to the two Universities had just been destroyed, thereby temporarily reducing the number of students and teachers.

Colleges had made some start in Italian and French Universities, but having no roots withered away. In England alone they continued to flourish, but in the year 1546 they were in imminent danger of destruction. Two years before, an Act of Parliament had been passed empowering the King to dissolve any chantry, college, hospital, etc., and appropriate its possessions. Greedy courtiers were now at their royal master's ears, urging him to use these powers at Oxford and Cambridge. It was high time, they thought, for the Colleges to go the way of the monasteries, that is to say for the Crown to seize their property and sell it at easy prices to the hangers-on of the Court.

In these circumstances the Cambridge authorities 'looked about them and made all the friends they could at court to save themselves'. In particular they urgently begged the aid of two of their professors, John Cheke, then acting as tutor to the prince of Wales, and Thomas Smith, then clerk to the queen's council. Parker tells us that the London friends of the University, among whom Smith and Cheke were doubtless conspicuous, wisely took the line of welcoming an enquiry, but begged the king to avoid the expense of a costly investigation. Their representations were successful, and he issued a commission dated 16 January 1546 to Mathew Parker (the vice-chancellor, and later archbishop of Canterbury), John Redman (warden of King's Hall, chaplain to the King, and later master of Trinity), and William Mey (president of Queens' and later archbishop-elect of York) to report to him on the revenues of the colleges and the number of students sustained therewith. The commissioners were capable and friendly. (*The King's Scholars and King's Hall*, 1917, p. 57.)

Indeed their report was so favourable to the Colleges and spoke so well of the use they were making of their then very moderate emoluments that King Henry swore 'he had not in his realm so many persons so honestly maintained in living by so little land and rent'.

One reason of this happy issue was that the Universities had found an influential advocate in Katharine Parr, Henry's sixth and last wife, the celebrated 'survivor'. She was a wise woman, and for her action in 1546 she deserves a statue in Cambridge and most of all in Trinity. She persuaded her formidable husband to spare the Colleges, which, as places of education for the clergy, could usefully be tuned to serve the purposes of the royal religion whatever it might be from time to time. Furthermore, Henry was persuaded to found a royal College of unprecedented size and magnificence. It should hold its own with his grandmother's foundation of St John's and with Christ Church, Oxford, the creation of that 'overgreat subject', the late Cardinal Wolsey. So far from adding the spoils of the Colleges to those of the convents, he would use monastic wealth to found a College which should be the bulwark of the new order of things.

And so King's Hall, with its royal connections, and its neighbour Michaelhouse were amalgamated in one College, which was further endowed with great quantities of land, tithe and advowsons recently taken from the monks. This new College, like King's College, was to fly the royal standard, and, unlike King's, its Master was to be appointed by the Crown, as he still is, alone among Cambridge Heads.*

It is to Henry's credit that he did not call his new foundation after his own name, but dedicated it to 'the Holy and Un-

* [The Master of Churchill College, founded in 1960, is also appointed by the Crown.]

divided Trinity'. It is, I hope, not unkind to suppose that he felt death near, as indeed it was. There was still one Spiritual Court which could summon a King of England, and perhaps he feared that he would soon have to plead before that impartial bar:

> In the corrupted currents of this world
> Offence's gilded hand may shove by justice,
> And oft 'tis seen the wicked prize itself
> Buys out the law: but 'tis not so above;
> There is no shuffling, there the action lies
> In his true nature; and we ourselves compelled,
> Even to the teeth and forehead of our faults
> To give in evidence.

Shakespeare put those words into the mouth of a king, and they represent an idea common in Tudor times; it may have affected even the self-willed Henry. His motives were probably mixed, in part political, in part pious. Whatever they were, this great deed of endowment closed and crowned his reign, which had been principally celebrated for actions of an opposite tendency.

The chief authorities for this pre-Trinity history are:

1. Willis and Clark, *Architectural History of the University of Cambridge*.
2. *The King's Scholars and King's Hall* (privately printed 1917), anonymous, but actually by Rouse Ball.
3. *Michaelhouse* (printed privately 1924 for the 600th anniversary).
4. Cooper's *Annals of Cambridge*.
5. *Cambridge Notes*, W. W. Rouse Ball (Heffer, 1921), being the 2nd edition of the work published by Macmillan in 1918 under the title *Cambridge Papers*.
6. *Admissions to Trinity College, Cambridge*, edited by W. W. Rouse Ball and J. A. Venn. Vol. I. (Macmillan, 1916.)
7. Mullinger, J. B., *The University of Cambridge* (3 vols.).
8. An unfinished MS. History of Trinity by Rev. A. H. F. Boughey (Dean, 1897–1908) in the College Library; full on the mediaeval history of King's Hall and Michaelhouse.
[9. A. B. Cobban, *The King's Hall within the University of Cambridge in the Later Middle Ages* (Cambridge 1969).
10. *Royal Commission on Historical Monuments. City of Cambridge* (H.M.S.O. 1959). These volumes, and those of Willis and Clark, also have much valuable information on later periods.]

NOTE ON PRIVATE HOSTELS

Several private hostels, of which the most important was Physwick's Hostel, stood on ground afterwards covered by the Great Court of Trinity.

Rouse Ball has thus described the origin and character of these establishments:

> The Colleges were originally intended for picked scholars. In the course of the fourteenth century the problem of the care of other students was taken up, and they were forbidden to live in lodgings selected by themselves and under no external supervision. To provide for them the University licensed private hostels. (*Cambridge Papers*, pp. 192–3.)
>
> Private Hostels were for the reception of Pensioners, i.e. of students who paid their own expenses, which for an average student came then to from £9 to £14 a year. A private hostel was managed by a master of arts who lived in it; it resembled in some respects a boarding-house at a modern public school, and maintained a continuous life. At the close of the medieval period there were seventeen of these hostels recognised in the University. Many of them belonged to Colleges who had purchased them as investments, and let them at a rack-rental. In the early part of the sixteenth century the number of students at Cambridge decreased, and the stress produced thereby fell heavily on the non-incorporated hostels. When the numbers of the University began to increase again, the Colleges admitted Pensioners, and the Private Hostels ceased to exist.
> (Rouse Ball, *Trinity College* (Dent, 1906), p. 39.)

CHAPTER II

THE EARLY DAYS OF TRINITY

MASTERS OF TRINITY

(Henry VIII) 1546: JOHN REDMAN
(Edward VI) 1551: WILLIAM BILL
(Mary)   1553: JOHN CHRISTOPHERSON
(Elizabeth) 1558: WILLIAM BILL (reinstated)
            1561: ROBERT BEAUMONT
            1567: JOHN WHITGIFT
       1577–93: JOHN STILL

TRINITY was, from the first, a very much richer society than King's Hall and Michaelhouse put together. Their joint endowments amounted to less than a quarter of those of Trinity, whose annual income as settled by Henry VIII was estimated at over £1600, a great sum in those days. Most of it was derived from land and endowments of parish churches that had belonged to dissolved monasteries, but some of the smaller estates made over to it had been purchased from private persons by the King.[1]

Not only the monasteries but the friaries had been dissolved, and one of the most interesting gifts made by Henry VIII to Trinity was the convent of the Franciscans or Grey Friars, occupying the future site of Sidney Sussex. The stones of the friary were used in the gradual construction of the new buildings of Trinity, until the sale to Sidney Sussex in 1596.

But though we so soon parted with the land of the Grey Friars, we still retain their water. The Franciscans had, in 1325, carried a fine supply from Conduit Head (on the Madingley Road), by pipes going underground and beneath

[1] The list of the original endowments of Trinity is printed at the end of Cooper's *Annals of Cambridge*, vol. I. There is some discrepancy between the figures there given, and those given in Rouse Ball's *Cambridge Papers* (Macmillan, 1918), pp. 10–12, 22.

the river, straight to their own convent in the middle of the town. As the pipe went through King's Hall territory, the Warden and scholars had had disputes with the friary, and had claimed to tap the water on its way through their grounds. In 1546 the pipe and the water, together with the rest of the possessions of the convent, passed into the hands of Trinity. In those days, before Hobson had brought his conduit into Cambridge, good water was rare and valuable. And even now, in these days of ample supply, the Franciscan water is still used for the College Fountain, whose splash at midnight has been grateful to the ears of so many generations of dwellers in the Great Court. Blessed be St Francis and his sister the water!*

In the first instance Trinity was filled up not only with members of the dissolved King's Hall and Michaelhouse, but with persons selected from the rest of the University, particularly from St John's. They were for the most part supporters of the new regime, trained in the new learning. Henry VIII chose Redman, a former Johnian, the last Warden of King's Hall, who was well known at Court, to be the first Master of Trinity, and nominated about sixty 'socii et scolares', who formed the original foundation. The numbers and the emoluments of the College steadily increased. Queen Mary provided more endowment, and under the Elizabethan statutes of 1560 there were to be sixty Fellows and sixty scholars (*discipuli*). And soon a large number of fellow-commoners and pensioners flocked to the new foundation, which rivalled St John's not only in size but in attractiveness to the 'new men' of the Tudor epoch. Gentry of moderate-sized estates or founders of legal families were taking the place of the old nobility as the real rulers of the land, partly because they did not despise education, but sent their sons to 'the learned Universities'. From the first the Trinity undergraduates were recruited from this modern element of well-to-do laymen, as well as from the older category of poor scholars aspiring to be priests.

In the reign of Elizabeth every member of the College under the degree of Master of Arts was required to have a Tutor.

* [Damage to the conduit pipe discovered during 1971 may prove irreparable, and other means may have to be discovered for supplying the Fountain with water.]

In this way privileged noblemen and fellow-commoners who dined at the Fellows' table, the ordinary pensioners, and the humblest sizars and sub-sizars were brought under the same rule as the scholars, the original members of the foundation. All were Trinity men together, subject to the same tutorial discipline and teaching. It was indeed reported to Lord Burghley as Chancellor of the University that some Tutors allowed greater licence to their richer pupils, who on the average were less studious and more gay. In those days differences of rank were universally recognised, even at the University, though College life had a valuable levelling and democratic influence.[1] In mediaeval times the ruling classes had eschewed and despised the University, but now their successors came there with the rest—greatly to the advantage of themselves and of the country; but they could not at once forgo all their privileges and all their easy manner of life, and had to be accepted more or less on that basis.

Tutors were not then, as they are now, College officers each dealing with large numbers of undergraduates. They were the ordinary Fellows taking two or three pupils each, by private arrangement with the pupils or their parents, or by order of the Master. The relationship was personal and close. The pupils often lived in the Tutor's rooms, for quarters were narrow in those days. The Master, from the time of Whitgift if not before, sometimes took pupils of his own into the Lodge. A man depended on his Tutor for advice about studies and for teaching: there was no one else to perform the functions of a modern supervisor or director of studies. The tutorial system was indeed the very essence of the College life. It was the method by which in Elizabeth's reign Trinity grew up to its first period of real greatness as a national institution.

[1] Although in Tudor and Stuart times some menial duties, subsequently abolished, were performed by sizars and sub-sizars, they always had the road of advancement to the top of the tree open to them. It is enough to say that Newton was a sub-sizar, and that Trinity never had a more favourite son. Bentley entered Cambridge as a sub-sizar of St John's.

Immediately after the death of the founder, the College received its first Statutes from his son Edward VI. Under Queen Mary new Statutes were drawn up but had not been sealed before she died. Their draft (*mutatis mutandis*) formed the basis of the Elizabethan Statutes which came into force in 1560, and remained, until the reign of Victoria, unaltered, though liberally 'interpreted' and often disregarded.

The Fellows were required to take Holy Orders and were not allowed to marry. Even the Master was by the Statutes forbidden to marry, but the custom grew up of obtaining leave from the King for him to take a wife to preside over the hospitality of the Lodge. John Still was a married man at the time he became Master in 1577. In 1672 Barrow's patent of Mastership from the Crown gave him permission to marry, but he caused it to be erased as contrary to the Statutes! In 1710 one of the official charges made by the Fellows against Bentley was that he had broken the Statutes by marrying and bringing his wife into the Lodge. But he successfully pleaded that he had first obtained the royal dispensation. After that, Masters were married more often than not.

But the Fellows could obtain no such exemption. Until they gave up their Fellowships, usually to take College livings, they could not marry. They remained a body of celibate clergymen, a kind of Protestant monastery, presiding somewhat incongruously over successive generations of high-spirited young men drawn from all ranks of society, who were by no means all of them destined for the Church, and very few of whom had any aspirations after the ascetic ideal. Such, until the later years of Queen Victoria, was the dual character of historic Trinity. Though ruled by clergymen there was nothing of the seminary about it. Mathematics, logic and classics were taught to the undergraduates, but little or no divinity. In such an institution the clerical and celibate character imposed upon the Fellows may seem to us to have been a mistake, a useless leave-over from the Middle Ages; yet the system worked pretty well, except during the eighteenth century.

The unmarried academic clergyman became a special type,

different from the parish priest. Some of the leading Trinity dons were in some respects very unclerical clergymen, such as Bentley in the eighteenth century, or Whewell and Adam Sedgwick in the nineteenth. Moreover there was always a lay element in the society, because a newly elected Fellow could postpone taking Orders for some few years, and certain Professorships could be held by laymen, as for instance by Newton.

From Tudor times till the new Statutes of 1882 the College was governed, not as now by a Council mainly elected by the general body of Fellows, but by the Master and the eight senior Fellows, known as the Seniority. Age was over-represented. And the Master's powers, even in relation to the Seniority, were very great.

In Tudor and Stuart times religion and religious disputes played a great part in the life of the College, where so many intending clergymen were being educated, at a time when the whole country was convulsed by the struggles of Catholic and Protestant, Puritan and Anglican. The second Master of Trinity, William Bill, refused to acquiesce in the Catholic reaction under Mary, and was forced to resign. But on Elizabeth's accession he was restored, in place of his Romanist supplanter, Christopherson, Bishop of Chichester. The first three Masters of Trinity, Redman, Bill and Christopherson, were all closely connected with the Court; they were all three able public men, who not only governed the infant society well, but guarded its interests with skill amid the treacherous and shifting quicksands of Tudor politics.

Fuller, in his *History of the University of Cambridge*, writes:

Queen Mary calling her chief clergy together, consulted with them about public prayers to be made for the soul of King Henry her father, conceiving his case not so desperate but capable of benefit thereby. They possessed her of the impossibility thereof, and that his holiness would never consent such honour should be done to one dying so notorious a schismatic. But they advised her in expression of her private affection to her father's memory, to add to Trinity College, (as the best monument he had left), whereon (chiefly at the instance of Bishop Christopherson) she bestowed £376. 10s. 3d. of yearly revenue.

In 1561, some three years after his restoration to the Mastership by Elizabeth, Bill died, and the Queen made an appointment which she soon regretted, in naming the Puritan Beaumont as his successor. In the early years of the reign the most influential man in Trinity and indeed in Cambridge was Cartwright, leader of the Presbyterian party which aimed at the abolition of Bishops and of the Prayer Book services. In 1565 the Puritans in the College broke all the windows in the Chapel 'wherein did appear superstition', and shortly afterwards the scholars, incited by three sermons preached on a single Sunday by Cartwright and two other Fellows, 'cast off their surplices as an abominable rag of superstition'.[1]

But the Puritan Master, Beaumont, was succeeded in 1567 by Whitgift, who, strong in the Queen's support, quelled religious insubordination in the royal College. He even succeeded in expelling Cartwright, on the ground that he had not taken priest's orders, a necessary condition of continued tenure of a Fellowship.

The check thus given to Puritanism in the College and University was of more than academic importance, for Cartwright was the national leader of a movement which in the first half of Elizabeth's reign bade fair to remould the still malleable features of the infant Church of England. Presbyterianism had strong support not only in the House of Commons but even among the Queen's Councillors. But she herself was staunch for the middle way in religion, and in 1577 called up Whitgift from the Mastership of Trinity to be Bishop of Worcester and a few years later Archbishop of Canterbury, to do to all England what he had done to our own College. Thus the great struggle of Anglican and Puritan, in which a man from Sidney Sussex was one day to take a hand, may almost be said to have originated, certainly to have been rehearsed, in the chambers and the Chapel of Trinity.

[1] Willis and Clark, II, 572; Rouse Ball, *Cambridge Papers*, pp. 92–3 and note; cf. Fuller's *History of the University of Cambridge*, pp. 265–6. ['Rag' is a slip for 'relic'.]

The building of the present Chapel had been begun in the reign of Mary Tudor and on her initiative. It was completed in the early years of her sister Elizabeth. It occupies the site of the old King's Hall Chapel, but covers about twice as much ground. Its Tudor-Gothic architecture recalls the decisive decade of the English Reformation, when the sad Queen Mary, who was so great a benefactor to our College, died frustrate, leaving it to her successor to dedicate England and Trinity to the ends and purposes she most abhorred.

But only the walls and roof of the Chapel are of Tudor origin. For the fine woodwork of the organ-screen, stalls, panels and the baldachino over the altar, we are indebted to Bentley and to his friends and enemies the Fellows in the reigns of Anne and the first two Georges. The elaborate scheme of mural decoration above*, and the coloured glass windows are patently Victorian.

The reign of Mary Tudor saw not only the beginning of the Chapel, but the erection of the first chambers of the new College, placed so as to connect the old buildings of King's Hall and Michaelhouse, now incorporate in Trinity. A Master's Lodge was built in two storeys, the walls of which constitute the present Parlour and Combination Room of the Fellows and the entrance hall and private drawing-room of the present Lodge. And this Master's Lodge was joined to the Edward III Gate, still in its old position where the sundial stands to-day, by a new row of College chambers (D in map, p. 2) that was pulled down forty years later when Nevile made the Great Court. But other chambers (E, E) which still survive were begun under Mary and completed under Elizabeth; they were built on either side of the Great Gate. That huge brick tower had hitherto stood isolated (see p. 7) but was now joined by new buildings (later Newton's staircase) to the Chapel on the north, and on the south was now connected by another new wing with the older row of King's Hall chambers (C) which has since disappeared.

The first buildings of Trinity proper were made very largely

* [The nineteenth-century paintings on the walls and ceiling of the Chapel, which had deteriorated badly, were painted over when the Chapel was redecorated in 1962–63.]

with the stone and lime brought from the ruins of the Franciscan convent. Even Mary Tudor could not prevent that; indeed the work was speeded in 1554 by a commission from 'Philipp and Marye by the grace of God Kyng and Queene of England', calling on all faithful subjects to assist the work. The Chapel was built with the stone partly of the Grey Friars in Cambridge, partly of Ramsey Abbey in the Fens.

NOTE

For the early history of Trinity see the authorities named at the end of Chapter I, especially Mullinger; and *Fellows of Trinity College*, a list compiled by H. McLeod Innes, 1941, with its valuable introductory matter.

CHAPTER III

NEVILE 1593–1615

The Great Court and the Cloisters

WHEN in February 1593 the ageing Queen Elizabeth, in a fortunate hour, appointed Thomas Nevile to succeed the innocuous John Still as Master of Trinity, the College over which he came to preside was, architecturally speaking, merely King's Hall and Michaelhouse strung together in an amorphous manner.[1] There was no indication of the Great Court, and meadow lands stretched over the site of the Cloisters. To one great man we owe them both. If Henry VIII founded Trinity, Nevile built it.

Nevile, as his name implies, came of a younger branch of an historic family. He was a Pembroke man in origin, had been Master of Magdalene, Vice-Chancellor in the Armada year, and held the Deanery of Peterborough till he changed it in 1597 for that of Canterbury. Strong in Court favour, and rich in ecclesiastical preferment, he devoted both his influence and his wealth to the making of Trinity. He never married, and he left to the College 'a bachelor's bounty'. Bishop Hacket, who had been under him at Trinity, wrote, 'He never had his like for a splendid, courteous and bountiful gentleman.'

It needed a man of unusual imagination, authority and strength of will to form and carry through his conception of the Great Court, for it meant not only new building on a magnificent scale, but the ruthless pulling down of many venerable relics of King's Hall, and of a modern wing in good

1 See map p. 22, which is a section of Hammond's map of Cambridge in 1592 (reproduced roughly in Willis and Clark, II, 402, and more exactly in Atkinson and Clark, *Cambridge described and illustrated*, 1897, p. 442). Hammond is more trustworthy than Lyne, who in his map of Cambridge in 1574 (Willis and Clark, II, p. 400) misplaces the Great Gate.

condition, erected by the Trinity men not forty years before. Only by such wholesale sacrifice, which must have had its

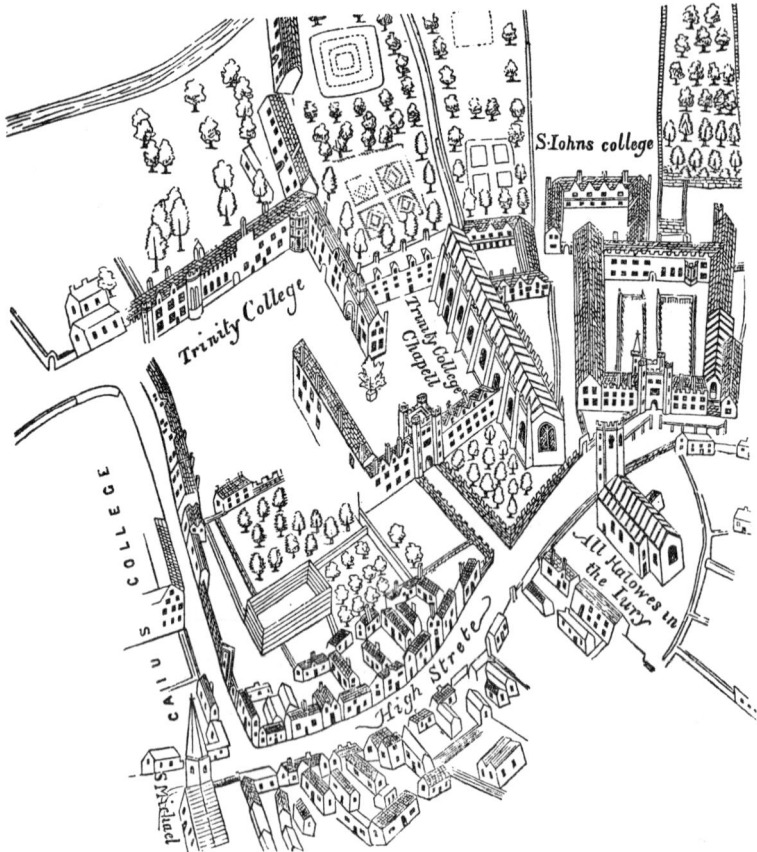

critics, could Nevile make clear the ample space of the Great Court.

Any ordinary man would have been content with a scheme, large enough in all conscience, which was occupying the mind of the College about the time when he became its Master. This rejected scheme is delineated in a map of which the original is still to be seen on the back staircase of our Library. (See Willis and Clark, II, 465-72, for reproduction of it and comment.) If this plan had been followed out, the Edward III Gate would have been left in its original position where the sundial stands to-day, with the two rows of chambers (B and D in map, p. 2) abutting on it from north and west; a new Library would have been built eastwards from the Edward III Gate to join it to the Great Gate, over land previously occupied by a wing of Robert de Croyland's house, leaving a second narrow court between this new Library and the Chapel. The rest of the Great Court would then have been completed much as now, but it would have been ninety feet shorter on the north: it would not have been clearly the finest College Court in the world. Later generations, even of Cambridge men, might have said that Tom Quad at Christ Church was finer.

This would not do for Nevile. Nothing should stand in the way of the great design he formed. He pulled down three wings of College buildings (B, C, and D, see p. 2) and he moved back the Edward III Gate (F) stone by stone to its present position in a line with the Chapel (G). With modern appliances such an operation would be relatively easy, though even now it would not be lightly undertaken. But in Elizabeth's reign the removal and re-erection of so large a fabric was an extraordinary feat. The statue of Edward III, with the inscriptions and coats of arms below it, was added at the same time, and a few years later a clock and bell. Thenceforth it was the College clock tower, though not with the present clock, which dates from 1726.*

This drastic shove-back of the north side of the projected Great Court involved building an entirely new north-west corner for it; this necessity Nevile turned to glorious gain, doubling the length and more than doubling the beauty of the Master's Lodge, and running a Library three storeys high† (I in map, p. 2) to join this extension of the Lodge to the Edward III clock tower in its new position. For seventy years the College books and manuscripts were housed in this new row of buildings,

* [The original clock is now in Orwell Church.]
† [Only the top floor of this three storey building seems to have been used as a Library.]

till Barrow employed Wren to give them a more princely home; after that Nevile's Library was adapted to serve as chambers.[1]

Nevile also removed a row of houses along the north side of the street now called Trinity Lane, in order to build the present south side of the Great Court with the Queen's Gate in the middle of it, adorned with the statue of Elizabeth. He completed the circuit of the Court by building the southern half of its east side; he decorated the north-west and south-east corners of the Court with the turrets that still remain. He erected the Fountain on its present site. And last but not least he replaced the decaying Michaelhouse buildings with the great Kitchen that still serves us,* and the Hall itself as we have it to-day.

Not content with this, in the last years of his life he built another Court, called after his name. The Cloisters of Nevile's Court, of which he built as much as two-thirds of the present length, were in a more Italianate or classical style than the Hall, whose west side formed the east end of the new Court. But the Cloisters then had gabled dormer windows of a more Gothic character, where the eighteenth-century balustrade now runs (see p. 70). The west side of Nevile's Court was left open, divided from the river meadows only by a low wall, until Wren's Library closed the gap. Beyond the wall, by the river side, a College tennis court was built in 1611, in place of an older one which had been removed to make room for the east side of the Great Court. These 'hard' enclosed tennis courts were elaborate structures. This one cost £120 to build—a large

[1] Nevile enriched the Trinity Library with some of its most valued treasures, which, as Dean of Canterbury, he took from the Cathedral Library and presented to Trinity. They include the Canterbury Psalter. Such removals ('*convey* the wise it call') were more tolerated in those days than they would be in ours, but even then it must have been a stretch of the Dean's authority. I expect that Whitgift, formerly Master of Trinity, who was Archbishop of Canterbury from 1583 to 1604, connived at Nevile's action in this matter. Whitgift himself transferred some Canterbury books to Trinity. But our greatest treasure is of later date—the MS. of many of Milton's minor poems in his own handwriting and with his own corrections.

* [A new Kitchen was constructed 1962–66. Nevile's kitchen survives as the 'Old Kitchen'.]

sum in the money of those days. There were no 'organised games' or boat races, but there was rough football—often little more than an excuse for a free fight with the Johnians—and archery; riding and fowling for the richer undergraduates, and walking for the poorer. Hobson the carrier, celebrated in two poems of somewhat elaborate conceits by young Mr Milton of Christ's, let out horses for travel and joy rides. Undergraduates had no option but to take the horse in the stall next the door; hence the expression 'Hobson's choice', which spread from Cambridge all over England.

Nevile paid for the Cloisters out of his own private fortune. But the expense of building the Great Court and Hall had been defrayed out of College funds or out of money raised by the College, £3000 of which Nevile had lent on easy terms. The Seniority had fallen in with the generous Master's plans; there was no such unseemly bickering about architectural improvements as raged a hundred years later between the grasping Bentley and the injured Fellows. Nevile presented to the College the beautiful 'Nevile Cup', which we still possess.

In one respect the Great Court as Nevile left it in 1615, and as it remained until the later years of the eighteenth century, was finer than it is to-day. On its west side (as can be seen from Loggan's print at the end of this book) there protruded three bays or oriels, reaching from ground to roof. Each differed in design from the other two; the Hall bay in the middle was polygonal; the Lodge bay to the north was semi-circular; the Kitchen bay to the south was a 'trefoil oriel' of three smaller semi-circles in a bunch. To-day only the oriel of the Hall remains, and its battlements have been altered for the worse. The trefoil oriel on the Kitchen wing disappeared when that portion of the Great Court was transformed in accordance with the severe taste of the later eighteenth century; and in the same spirit the semi-circular oriel of the Lodge was removed, to be restored in a polygonal form by Whewell in the period of the Gothic revival.

Fortunately, however, the Hall itself has been little altered since it was first built in 1604. Its east and west oriels looking out on the two Courts, the tiers of arches decorating the rafters, the elaborate woodwork of the screen and minstrels' gallery, the panelling above the dais at the north end, the beautiful lantern on the roof outside, are all as Nevile left them. The panels along the east and west sides of the Hall have indeed been renewed, but on the old pattern. Until the nineteenth century the only heating of the Hall came from a brazier in the middle, the lantern above being left open for the fumes to escape. The brazier is now preserved in the courtyard behind the Combination Room.

After the sale of the land and ruins of the former Franciscan convent to the new College of Sidney Sussex in 1596, the stone for Nevile's building operations could no longer come from the Grey Friars. Various other sources were tapped, some of not very high quality. Local quarries could only supply clunch, the 'white stone' which was brought from the chalk pits at Cherry Hinton, Barrington and Eversden. It can still be seen in the walls of Nevile's part of the Lodge that face the Master's garden, side by side with the bricks used a hundred years later by Bentley when he made his alterations. Nevile seems to have despised brick, though it had been used by the builders of the Great Gate. He obtained 'rag' stone from Cambridge Castle, then in gradual process of demolition. And he brought better stone from Northamptonshire, probably by water most of the way. It was partly on account of the inferior character of some of the stone he used that both then and afterwards much of the Great Court was encased with stucco. Later generations have refaced a good deal of it with better stone (see p. 69, below).

Indeed much of Nevile's work was by no means as solid as it was beautiful. Thus in Bentley's time it was found necessary to rebuild the Fountain, but fortunately the design of the Jacobean carving was followed with very little change. It is a curious fact that the Fountain when first built by Nevile had been painted, perhaps to preserve stone of indifferent quality.

Nevile, put up the statue of Henry VIII over the outer

entrance of the Great Gate. On the inner side, the statues of James I and his wife Anne of Denmark, and their only surviving son Prince Charles, were erected in 1615, the year when Nevile died. They commemorate two royal visits to Trinity made in March and May of that year, when the King and the Prince had with great content seen Latin and English plays enacted in the Hall, had gone to service in the Chapel, and slept in the Master's Lodge.[1]

The custom was thus established that royal visitors to Cambridge should put up at Trinity. Similarly Nevile's personal friendship with the greatest of all Trinity and of all English Judges, Sir Edward Coke, is said to have been the reason why the King's Judges on Assize have ever since been housed in the Master's Lodge of Coke's old College. The accounts of the Trinity Steward show that Coke stayed in the College in 1610 and 1612 when on circuit. There is no evidence that any Judge before him had been so entertained. Sometimes in Elizabeth's reign the Judges on Assize had slept in inns in the town. After Coke's time they slept in Trinity.[2]

In William III's reign Justice Rokeby, in his diary for March 12, 1694/5, thus describes his departure from the Lodge:

The coach could not conveniently go into Trinity College where I lay, so the Sheriff provided me a chair which carried me through the College to the coach.

Nevile's Gate, which now leads out of Trinity Lane into Bishop's Hostel, was probably built by the great Master him-

[1] Willis and Clark, II, 487, 510; Cooper's *Annals of Cambridge*, III, 66–86.

[2] It is not true, though it has sometimes been stated, that Trinity Lodge is a royal palace, in which the Sovereign and his Judges have the legal right to stay as in their own house. It is a matter of concession and custom, not law. The customary rights conceded to the Judges by the College were defined in an Instrument agreed to by all parties in the year 1866. The question whether the Judge's customary rights in the Lodge had also a legal basis was left undecided in this Instrument. The College holds the negative view. An historical review of the whole question by the Vice-master, Mr Winstanley, is lodged in the College Office. [Now more conveniently available in D. A. Winstanley *Later Victorian Cambridge* (Cambridge 1947). The Assize Judge ceased to visit Cambridge in 1971.)

self in the reign of James I. It stood originally in the middle of the wall that then divided Nevile's Court from the river meadows to the west. When, in Charles II's reign, Wren's Library was built on that site, the Gate was transferred to the head of the newly planted lime avenue beyond the river, where it appears in Loggan's print. Finally it was moved to its present position in 1876, during the Mastership of W. H. Thompson, whose arms, with those of his wife, were then added to the arms of Nevile and his relations that adorn the gate.

The Master's Lodge as we now have it is the work of Nevile, altered by Bentley, re-altered by Whewell and finally extended under Montagu Butler. The older part of the Lodge, dating from 1554, included some, if not all, of the space now occupied by the Parlour and Combination Room of the Fellows. It also included the present entrance hall of the Lodge, which still has some old Tudor panelling, and the small drawing-room overhead. I have already told how Nevile doubled the length northward of the old Lodge in course of constructing the north-west corner of the Great Court. In so doing he built the present dining-room and Judge's bedrooms on the ground floor, and the Tudor drawing-room and royal bedrooms above.

The Tudor drawing-room still displays unchanged the glory of Nevile's decorations: the embossed ceiling of plasterwork picked out with gold is a fair rival to the ceiling of the Combination Room of St John's; the highly ornamented and coloured fireplace shows the emblazoned arms of Queen Elizabeth, supported by the lion of England and the dragon of Wales, for the Tudors were a Welsh family; it was only James I who introduced the unicorn, that used to support the arms of Scotland, to show the union of the English and Scottish Crowns in the person of the new Sovereign. Below the royal arms is the shield of the College, with that of Nevile (a St Andrew's cross) on one side, and on the other the arms of the former Master, Whitgift, as Archbishop of Canterbury.[1]

[1] Willis and Clark (II, 620) are mistaken in saying that the arms are those of the Deanery of Canterbury, then held by Nevile. They are

THE GREAT COURT AND THE CLOISTERS

The other rooms which Nevile added to the Lodge completely changed their appearance when Bentley in Queen Anne's reign panelled the dining-room and the King's and Judges' bedrooms. When in 1941 the panels of the dining-room were taken down for repair, Nevile's fireplace was revealed, built of clunch a few feet to the north of the present fireplace. At the same time traces of red line painting were found on the plaster of the walls, probably the remains of the original wall decorations of the dining-room by Nevile.

In those days there was another part of the Lodge running westwards towards the river. The eastern end of this western wing of the Lodge has now been replaced by the red brick wing built in Montagu Butler's time. The farther part, nearer the river, was the Comedy Room where, in Elizabethan and Stuart times, the undergraduates acted Latin and English plays at Christmastide. When very large audiences were invited, the Hall was used. In Nevile's day there was a good deal of play acting and play writing by Trinity men.

This Comedy Room was a high, long, narrow building, older than the rest of the College. In the fourteenth century it had been a private house of stone, stretching along the side of King's Childers Lane towards the landing-place on the river (*H* in map; see note, p. 1 above). It was pulled down in the first decade of the nineteenth century. Its south wall, patched with the bricks of six succeeding centuries, is all that now remains of it, forming the south wall of the Master's garden; in it the ancient doors and windows can still be traced by the curious. The bees have made their hive in a blocked-up window that witnessed the Wars of the Roses; a giant fig-tree stretches up over a Tudor mullion. Through those windows the scholars of lost years looked out, in the intervals of rehearsing Plautus and Terence, or living authors like Ben

the personal arms of Whitgift (a cross with balls) and the pallium as the symbol of the Archbishopric which he held when Nevile made the fireplace, viz. in 1600 or a few years later. Similarly Nevile put up his own and Whitgift's arms under the statue of Elizabeth on the Queen's Gate where they can still be seen.

Jonson and Shakespeare, or dearer still to the young actors, the ingenious products of their own academic wit (see note at end of chapter).

Under Whitgift and Nevile, Trinity, which had originated almost as a 'colony' of John's,[1] became its rival on equal terms. In those days rivalry meant enmity. The Trinity undergraduates fought 'the St John's pigs' (*porci*), with fists and clubs, as frequently and as fiercely as they fought the townees. In the early and middle Tudor period Lady Margaret's Foundation had led the University in the new learning, in the days when its great scholars 'taught Cambridge, and King Edward, Greek'; St John's attracted the 'new men' who led the country in place of the old feudal nobility. William Cecil, Lord Burghley, had been a Johnian, and so was his son Robert Earl of Salisbury.

But in Elizabeth's reign, Trinity also began to educate a large proportion of the leaders of the new era. Edward Coke came up in 1567 at the age of fifteen, and Francis Bacon in 1573 at the age of twelve: the devotion of the great lawyer-politician and the great lawyer-philosopher to their College and University was life-long. In January 1579 Whitgift took in to the Lodge as his own pupil the Earl of Essex, then aged twelve, already under the personal patronage of the Queen and of Burghley. In his brilliant and tragic career he never lost sight of Trinity and Cambridge. He became Chancellor of the University, and presented 'the Essex cup' for the use of successive Vice-Chancellors. Our Hall contains fine contemporary portraits of Essex and of Bacon, the generous and headstrong patrician and his calculating friend.

[1] In the year 1570 Roger Ascham wrote in his *Scholemaster*, 'Yea, St. Johne's did then so flourish, as Trinity College, that princely house now, at the first erection was but *colonia deducta* out of St. Johne's, not onlie for their master, fellowes, and scholers, but also, which is more, for their whole both order of learning and discipline of maners'. For details corroborating this statement, see Mullinger, *University of Cambridge*, II, 84–5.

The early age at which these great men came up to Trinity will be noted. The undergraduate society was still composed half of boys and half of young men. Some of the rules and corporal punishments were meant for the boys only, but tact must have been required in exercising discipline over a society that was still a straddle between a public school and a College. The close relationship of the Tutor to his pupil, who often resided in his rooms, may have helped in the management of the younger boys.

Another man of high family and Court connection, George Herbert, was sixteen when he came up as pensioner in 1609. The religious, literary and musical life of Nevile's Trinity enchanted Herbert's eager mind and diverted it from a worldly career: he became poet, parson and saint instead of courtier and statesman. The Victorian stained glass in our ante-Chapel is not good, but its designer had a good thought when, in one of the New Testament scenes, he put the gentle George Herbert, in his habit as he lived, standing behind the seated figure of our Lord.[1]

Another man of religion was at Trinity under Nevile, John Winthrop, 'the Moses of New England'. The Winthrop family was closely connected with the College, and John was here from 1602 to 1605, aged fourteen to seventeen. A Puritan lad like Winthrop did not feel out of place at Trinity, where there was still a strong party of that way of thinking, though no longer predominant since Whitgift had driven out Cartwright thirty years before. Indeed, when yet another thirty years had passed, it was reported to the Oxford busy-body then occupying the see of Canterbury, that at Trinity, Cambridge, 'in some tutors' chambers the private prayers are longer and louder by far at night than they are at Chapel in the evening'. At Chapel indeed 'they lean, or sit or kneel at

[1] Trinity was rich in poets in the first half of the seventeenth century. Besides Herbert, Abraham Cowley matriculated scholar, aged nineteen, in 1637; Andrew Marvell, sizar in 1633, aged twelve, became scholar in 1638; finally John Dryden was a Westminster scholar of the 1650 election, aged nineteen. [The stained glass was removed from the Ante-Chapel in 1948-9; Herbert appears in a window of the Chapel.]

prayers, every one in a several posture as he pleases. At the name of Jesus few will bow, and when the creed is repeated, many of the boyes, by some men's directions, turn towards the west door'.

However, these recalcitrants had not got it all their own way. In that same year 1636 the High Church party redecorated the Chapel in a manner that seemed to the Puritans 'superstitious' (Rouse Ball, *Cambridge Papers*, pp. 95–6).

But the rival parties in the College would soon be annoying one another by ways more serious than turning to the west during the creed or railing off the altar. Nevile had been twenty years dead; and the first golden age of Trinity was fading fast, as golden ages will. The English sky was darkening with the approach of the greatest storm of our domestic history. Andrew Marvell of Trinity would soon have reason to write:

> The forward youth that would appear
> Must now forsake his Muses dear,
>   Nor in the shadows sing
>   His numbers languishing,
> 'Tis time to leave the books in dust
> And oil the unused armour's rust;
>   Removing from the wall
>   The corselet of the hall.

Note on the Comedy Room
(see p. 29 above)

The Comedy Room, of which the southern wall of the Master's garden represents the only remaining part, was certainly not built by Nevile (as Willis and Clark tentatively suggest, II, 605, map, and 622). He may indeed have altered or adapted it and very probably added the lantern on the roof shown in Loggan's print below. But most of the stone work of its remaining wall is mediaeval, as Mr A. W. Clapham, Secretary of the Royal Commission on Historical Monuments, told me after examining it in March 1941. In Hammond's pre-Nevile map of 1592 (p. 22, above) a house is marked running down towards the river along King's Childers Lane just at that angle.

MASTERS OF TRINITY AFTER NEVILE
1615: JOHN RICHARDSON
1625: LEONARD MAWE
1629: SAMUEL BROOKE
1631–45: THOMAS COMBER

CHAPTER IV

HOW TRINITY MADE THE BEST OF TWENTY TROUBLOUS YEARS: 1642–1662

MASTERS OF TRINITY

1631: THOMAS COMBER
1645: THOMAS HILL
1653: JOHN ARROWSMITH
1659: JOHN WILKINS (first Secretary of
 The Royal Society, 1662)
1660: HENRY FERNE

OLIVER CROMWELL at the age of seventeen had been an undergraduate of Sidney Sussex, but he had not acquired the academic bent of mind. A quarter of a century had passed since then, and he was now a middle-aged family man, a gentleman grazier, resident at Ely. He was popular with the fenmen, whose interests he had voiced against the indifference of 'the great' in the matter of the drainage awards. And 'when civil dudgeon first grew high' he had been chosen to sit for Cambridge Borough in the two successive Parliaments that met in 1640.

Two years later his brother-members, smelling powder in the air, very wisely sent him down from Westminster to his own countryside to support there the authority of the Houses against the King. In a region where there was no great territorial magnate to take the lead, a plain squire of daemonic energy, armed with the mandate of Parliament and trusted by his neighbours, could quickly raise force enough to make him practical ruler of the county, and enable him to deal with the Fellows of Colleges very much as he wished.

The first conflict of wills was over the silver plate, which a number of Colleges, including Trinity, were designing to send to the King at York. Colonel Cromwell was able to stop all, or nearly all, before it left Cambridge. The old 'Town and

Gown' feeling ran higher than ever, fused now with the issues of national politics. The majority of the dons and undergraduates were for the King, and the majority of the townsmen for Parliament; the presence of the troops which Cromwell had raised decided the balance of power. But the Colleges, unwilling to submit tamely, ordered fifteen chestfuls of weapons from London for their own defence; the Mayor however secured ten of them, 'but the scholars of Trinity College had first taken five of them before the Mayor knew thereof'.[1]

The University soon abandoned further resistance. Cambridge became the military headquarters of the Eastern Association, the area of which included just the same counties as the Eastern Defence Region during the War of 1939-45. Parliament, owing to the genius of Cromwell, was able to prevent the greater part of this region from becoming the seat of war. The University, therefore, unlike Oxford which stood a siege, saw nothing of actual fighting, but had soldiers quartered in it, and was subjected to a rule it disliked.

Materially Trinity suffered very little. Our College bridge, among others, was demolished as part of a scheme of defence for the town, but was rebuilt in 1651.[2] In the Chapel, the High Church changes of a few years before were reversed, and the communion table moved back from the east end into the middle. The notorious iconoclast, William Dowsing, could find little more to do in Trinity Chapel. 'We had four cherubims and steps levelled' is the most he can say in his *Journal*—a disappointing haul, though better here than at Puritan Emmanuel, where there was nothing that even Dowsing could find to destroy.

---

[1] Cooper, *Annals of Cambridge*, III, 326. For this period see *passim* Cooper, *Annals*; Mullinger, *University of Cambridge*; and Fuller's *History of the University of Cambridge*. See F. J. Varley, *Cambridge during the Civil War* (Heffer, 1935), chapter VII, on Cromwell and the College plate.

[2] The bridge as rebuilt in 1651 is delineated in Loggan's print. The present bridge which replaced it in 1765 bears the arms of the College and those of Dr Hooper, who left the money with which it was built.

It was a blessing that this deplorable man was not allowed to work his will on the glass of King's College Chapel, though the edifice was used by the soldiers as a drill hall. Perhaps Colonel Cromwell kept Master Dowsing in order. All Puritans were not equally savage in their iconoclasm. Mr Milton of Christ's had only recently written in praise of

> Storied windows, richly dight,
> casting a dimm religious light.

Or perhaps Oliver remembered that the windows in King's had been set there by Henry VIII, an Englishman, by whom, though only half enlightened, God had wrought mightily in his day.[1]

The Civil War and its aftermath of persecutions and the reaction of 1662 were necessarily injurious to academic society, implying alternate 'purges' first of those who refused to take the Covenant, and then of those who refused to accept the restored Prayer Book. But the 'forcers of conscience' were the London politicians, not the academic body itself. Indeed, the most remarkable thing about the internal history of the University and the Colleges from 1642 to the Revolution of 1688 and after, is the relative absence of political and religious bitterness. The High Church party was never so fanatical here as at Oxford, either in the time of Laud or after the Restoration. And Puritan fanaticism was rather imposed from outside than bred within.

At Trinity the first purge drove out more than forty 'uncovenanted' Fellows, including Abraham Cowley the poet, Humphry Babington of Rothley Temple in Leicestershire, and Thomas Sclater. Babington and Sclater returned at the Restoration and became benefactors of the College, completing the Cloisters of Nevile's Court to stretch as far as the new Library. Sclater became a Baronet, and as a county magistrate in Charles II's reign, the good 'Sir Thomas' was

[1] In chapter IV of Varley's *Cambridge in the Civil War* it is argued that the amount of glass destroyed by Dowsing in East Anglia has been exaggerated. The 'superstitious pictures' which he boasts of removing were real pictures in most cases, not glass.

famous for his humane discouragement of informers and his kindness to Puritan nonconformists, in spite of all that he himself had suffered. His portrait hangs at the top of our Library staircase.

In 1645 Comber, the first Master of any distinction since Nevile, was turned out for refusing the Covenant, and had not the good fortune to live till the Restoration. His kindly and jovial features, his hirsute beard and moustache, and his old-fashioned ruff and skull-cap, give a pleasant idea of him in the portrait now hanging in the entrance hall of the Lodge. He had been no maker of strife, and he suffered for no fault of his own.

Throughout the whole of this period, undisturbed by all its changes, two purely academic movements, the one of religious thought and the other of mundane learning, went forward at Cambridge: one was the Cambridge Platonists, the other the 'natural philosophers' (or as we should now call them the 'scientists').* These two forms of spiritual and mental activity built a bridge between opposing parties in religion, and gave scholars something better to think about than the barren polemics of ecclesiastical hatred.

In both movements Trinity played its part. The leading Cambridge Platonists, Whichcote and John Smith, were indeed men of other Colleges, and were Puritan in affinity, but a prelude to the whole movement has been traced in the discourse or 'common-place' delivered in our Chapel by John Sherman, Fellow of Trinity, under the aegis of the moderate Anglican Master, Comber. The Cambridge Platonists wedded an earnest Christianity to a reasonable philosophy connected with that of the ancient Greeks. Sherman's discourse was entitled 'A Greek in the Temple' and was printed in 1641.[1]

But in the new movement of 'natural philosophy' Trinity during the period of the Commonwealth assumed a leadership

[1] See the College Library for the original; also see Mullinger, III, 588–9, who emphasises Sherman's connection with the Platonists. For the whole movement see chapter VII of Basil Willey's *Seventeenth Century Background*. Our John Sherman is not to be confused with a younger John Sherman of Queens' and Jesus, who wrote the History of Jesus College.

* [According to the O.E.D. the word scientist was first used by Whewell in his *Philosophy of the Inductive Sciences* in 1840.]

that it has never since lost. John Ray, the great naturalist and botanist, was a Fellow of Trinity. He resigned his Fellowship in 1662 rather than accept the precise wording of the new Anglican oaths, although he remained till his death in 1705 in communion with the Established Church whose tests he had refused to his own hurt. In such combined moderation and scrupulosity there is the same spirit that was found again two hundred years later in Henry Sidgwick. Ray and his pupil Willughby, another Trinity man, did much to make natural history a science, and the beautiful busts of them by Roubiliac at the entrance of the College Library form a worthy memorial of their fruitful friendship. 'In their deaths they are not divided.' (See *John Ray*, by Prof. Raven, Camb. Univ. Press, 1942.)

The last of the Roundhead Masters of Trinity was John Wilkins, first Secretary of the Royal Society when that body was founded in 1662. He also was a 'moderate', but unlike Ray he conformed at the Restoration and became a Bishop.

Then too there was Isaac Barrow, the great mathematician and eloquent preacher of a humane and enlightened Christianity. In the last years of the Commonwealth he brought out his edition of *Euclid*, as a young Fellow of twenty-five;[1] since he was even then an avowed Royalist, yet continued to hold his Fellowship by the protection of the Master, there were evidently strict limits to Puritan intolerance in Trinity!

Such then was the atmosphere of the College when, in 1661, Isaac Newton at the age of eighteen matriculated as a subsizar. He did not enter a society torn by rival fanaticisms. Its prevalent tone, both before and after the Restoration, was moderation in politics, interest in scientific and mathematical study, and earnest but philosophical religion. These surroundings did much to decide the bent of Newton's mind in all its aspects.

[1] In the dining-room of the Lodge there is a portrait of him as a very young man, in the dress of the Commonwealth period, holding his *Euclid* open in his hand.

CHAPTER V

RESTORATION TRINITY

BARROW   NEWTON   THE LIBRARY

MASTERS OF TRINITY

	1659: JOHN WILKINS
(Charles II)	1660: HENRY FERNE
	1662: JOHN PEARSON
	1672: ISAAC BARROW
	1677: HON. JOHN NORTH
(James II, William III)	1683–1699: HON. JOHN MONTAGU

THE REIGN of Charles II was another great period for Trinity, marked by Isaac Newton's residence in the College, the Masterships of Pearson and Barrow, and the building of the Library.

Though an Anglican purge of the society took place after the Restoration, cancelling the Puritan purges of the last twenty years, not a few of the former Roundhead Fellows were retained or formally readmitted.[1] The higher intellectual life of the College moved forward without interruption. The change from Roundhead to Royalist rule was bridged by the presence of Isaac Barrow, equally great as a mathematician and as a divine. In both spheres of his activity he received notable aid. In 1661 Isaac Newton came up as a sub-sizar, and next year Pearson, one of the most renowned Fathers of Anglican Theology ('Pearson on the Creed'), became Master of the College.

During the critical period of transition that followed the death of Cromwell, the College was particularly fortunate in its Heads. In those days the Master's authority was very great, and a political zealot might have done untold harm to the

[1] For an account of the ejections and restorations of Fellows between 1642 and 1662 see McLeod Innes' *Fellows of Trinity, Cambridge* (1941), pp. 11–13, and the lists that follow.

peculiar ethos of Trinity. But Wilkins, Ferne and Pearson, who occupied the Lodge in rapid succession during the years 1659–62, were all moderate in temper, men of humanity and tact. Wilkins accepted the Restoration and might have continued as Master, but for the circumstance that Charles I had granted a patent of the Mastership in reversion to Henry Ferne, his faithful chaplain in the days of misfortune. Wilkins, therefore, retired, to become the first Secretary of the Royal Society in 1662, and six years later Bishop of Chester. Ferne, after a brief reign in which he did much to heal the open wounds of College life, died in March 1662, and was succeeded by Pearson.

The ten years of Pearson's beneficent rule were notable for the rapid rise to eminence in the University of the young Newton. Barrow was his teacher. In 1663 Barrow, who had before been Regius Professor of Greek, was appointed the first Lucasian Professor of Mathematics. But so strong was his impression of his pupil's genius, and such was his own generosity and unselfishness, that after holding the Mathematical Professorship for six years he deliberately resigned it in order that it should be held by Newton, then a young man of twenty-six. It was a transaction which reflected honour on the College that bred them both. Another three years passed before Barrow succeeded Pearson as Master.

Newton's whole academic life, from 1661 to 1696, was spent at Trinity. In 1667 he became a Fellow, and retained his Fellowship in spite of the fact that he remained a layman, because Charles II provided by Letters Patent that the Lucasian Professor even if not in Holy Orders might continue to hold a Fellowship, notwithstanding any College Statute to the contrary (*University Commission Report*, 1852, p. 57).

For long (how long we do not know) Newton lived in E 4 Great Court, the rooms on the first floor between the Chapel and the Great Gate, on the side next to the Gate.[1]

---

[1] See Appendix C of Winstanley's *Early Victorian Cambridge*, pp. 434–5. The staircase is a good one: Macaulay occupied the ground-floor rooms next the Chapel, and Thackeray the set opposite, since taken in to be part of the Porter's Lodge. Rooms on the staircase were occupied by Lightfoot, Jebb, and Frazer of the *Golden Bough*. Newton's

He was certainly there in 1687 when he brought out his *Principia*, possibly the most important scientific work ever published, not excepting the *Origin of Species* by Darwin of Christ's. But Newton had been pursuing the argument of the *Principia* for twenty years before publication; indeed his speculations on the power of gravity reached an important stage in the year 1665, when he was twenty-three years of age, not yet either Fellow or Professor. Those who, with Professor Hardy*, believe that men of science and mathematicians have their best period of inspiration at least as early as poets, can quote the case of Newton. Within the ten years following the publication of the *Principia* the mind of the world's greatest scientist turned away from science, partly because of the strain his studies put upon his health. His interest veered round to biblical exegesis and public service. In 1696, at the age of fifty-three, he left Trinity, never to return as a resident. He went to assist the Government of William III in the difficult and dangerous operation of the re-coinage.[1] He had been summoned to preside over it by the Chancellor of the Exchequer, his friend Charles Montagu (afterwards Earl of Halifax), the Trinity man to whom England largely owes her modern financial system, the Bank of England, and the National Debt.

Newton never again left the public service. He remained in London as Master of the Mint till his death in 1727. Trinity saw him no more except as an occasional visitor. He was therefore able to avoid taking sides in the discreditable feuds that rent the College during the Mastership of Bentley in the reigns of Anne and George I.

Newton, like his friend Montagu, was a moderate Whig, of the post-Revolution, not of the Popish Plot, type. As such the University chose him as one of its Members in the Convention Parliament that settled the Constitution in 1689, and again in the less celebrated assembly of 1701-2.

What was Newton like as a member of the College society? There is singularly little tradition. The picture of him in the

rooms are those now occupied by Professor Broad (1942). [Professor Broad died in 1971. Lord Adrian had preceded him in Newton's rooms.]

[1] Clearly and fully described in Macaulay's *History of England*.

* [Trevelyan is referring to G. H. Hardy, *A Mathematician's Apology*.]

drawing-room of the Lodge, wigless and in his dressing-gown, painted for Bentley by Thornhill in 1710, confirms the impression from other sources of a quiet, serious, sharp-faced man, not to be trifled with, but without either shyness or arrogance. Loggan's print at the end of this book shows Newton's enclosed garden (at the east end of the Chapel) and the wooden staircase leading down into it from his rooms next the Great Gate. The land is now an open grass plot. It was there that the greatest of Trinity men used to walk, in lonely and concentrated thought.*

Charles II who, no less than our royal founder, 'loved a man', had often conversed with Barrow, and heard him preach as one of the royal chaplains. In 1672 he appointed him to succeed Pearson in the Mastership, saying he 'gave it to the best scholar in England'. Charles was a cynic, but he was capable of appreciating goodness on the somewhat rare occasions when it came his way, witness his appointment of Ken to the Bishopric of Bath and Wells in spite of, or because of, the uncourtierly firmness with which Ken had 'refused poor Nelly a lodging' in his prebendal house in the Close at Winchester. So, too, the appointment of Barrow, we are told, was 'the King's own act'. It had not been solicited.

After five years in the Master's Lodge, Barrow died, at the early age of forty-seven, leaving a composite reputation as mathematician, preacher, classic and theologian, which lasted for two centuries, but has now receded into the dimmer past as happens to the fame of all save the very greatest. When I came up to Trinity in 1893, not only were the statues of Bacon and Barrow on each side of Newton in the ante-Chapel, as they still are†, but portraits of the same trio were hung as the only pictures at the north end of the Hall above the dais, where Henry VIII in all his glory has now superseded them.[1]

---

[1] When the huge picture of Henry VIII was moved from the Lodge drawing-room to the Hall in Montagu Butler's time, the Master remarked 'it took six men to carry him, one for each of his wives'.

* [In 1954 an apple tree, descended from one at Newton's home, Woolsthorpe Manor, was planted here.]

† [The statues were re-arranged 1948–49, and Newton's now stands on its own at the west end.]

Barrow is no longer thought of in a class with Bacon and Newton, but he is still remembered next to Nevile as the maker of the Trinity we know, for he was the only begetter of Wren's Library on the river bank.

The finest of our buildings was most admirably placed, its west side adorning the Backs, and its east side completing Nevile's Court (see p. 24 above). The two restored Royalist Fellows, Sclater and Babington (see p. 36 above), paid for the further extension westward of the Cloisters to join the new Library. The glimpse we get, through the grills, of the Cloister Court from the Backs, and of the Backs from the Cloister Court, is a stroke of Wren's genius. His somewhat similar Library at The Queen's College, Oxford*, has been spoiled by subsequent blocking-up of the ground floor, I suppose for utilitarian purposes.

It was Barrow who persuaded his friend Sir Christopher to design our Library. The great architect gave us his services gratis, and we commemorate him as one of our Benefactors. He took infinite pains, producing first a design for a building with a cupola, not wholly unlike the circular Library at Oxford by his pupil Gibbs, but not so good. The drawing for it is preserved in All Souls and is reproduced in Rouse Ball's *Cambridge Papers*, Chapter VIII. When this first design was rejected he worked out his actual masterpiece, not without several further changes of plan. The material that he chose was stone with an occasional tinge of pink colour, from the quarry of Ketton on the borders of Northamptonshire and Rutland. The quarry was afterwards closed, I believe for some 150 years; but it has been re-opened in our own day in connection with Ketton cement, and the College has recently used Ketton stone in repairs in the Great Court, to reface Newton's staircase and parts of the Hall. It has also been used for Herbert Baker's new buildings at Downing.

The riverside ground on which the Library was to stand offered no firm foundation. Wood piles were therefore driven into the soggy soil to support each of the pillars. That is the reason why the floor level below the pillars is to-day higher than

---

* [The Library at The Queen's College is not by Wren; the architect was perhaps Henry Aldrich (1648–1710), Dean of Christ Church, and architect of Peckwater Quadrangle there. W. G. Hiscock, *A Christ Church Miscellany* (Oxford 1946), pp. 26–9.]

some of the surrounding flagstones which have sunk, because, though they bear no weight, they have no piles beneath them.*

Wren was as much interested in the interior as in the exterior of the Library, and he secured equal splendour for both by a peculiar architectural device. Seen from the outside the building appears to consist of two storeys of equal height. But actually the floor of the Library rests half-way down the lower storey, thus giving greater height to the interior. In the beautifully proportioned room thus obtained, Wren designed the tall shelves down the sides, which are its most striking feature. Grinling Gibbons himself did the ornamental woodwork; the coats of arms that he carved at the ends of the shelves are those of the principal subscribers to the cost of building the Library. A list of the subscribers' names and the amount of their gifts occupies five large pages of Cooper's *Memorials of Cambridge* (1861, II, 266–72). In 1695 after the Library had been completed, the subscription list was closed; it had by then amounted to £11,879. 2s. 1d. It had unfortunately been thought necessary to sell a large quantity of our old plate to find more money for the building (Conclusion Book, Nov. 18, 1679, and Jan. 15, 1679/80).

Barrow dying in 1677 never saw the interior or the roof of the Library that we owe to him. In the Life of his successor, 'the Hon. Dr John North', written by his brother Roger North, occurs the following celebrated passage:

> When the doctor entered upon the mastership of Trinity College, the building of the great Library, begun by his immediate predecessor, Dr Barrow, was advanced about three-quarters of the height of the outward wall; and the doctor most heartily and diligently applied his best forces towards carrying it on; and, besides his own contributions, most of his friends and relations, upon his encouragement, became benefactors; the particulars thereof will appear in the accounts of that noble structure. The tradition of this undertaking runs thus. They say that Dr Barrow pressed the heads of the university to build a theatre, it being a profanation and scandal that the speeches should be had in the university church, and that also be deformed with scaffolds, and defiled with rude crowds

---

* [The Library rests not on piles but on a series of inverted brick arches built over a raft of clunch some twelve feet below ground level. The paving beneath the Library was levelled in the restoration completed in 1971.]

and outcries. This matter was formally considered at a council of the heads; and arguments of difficulty, and want of supplies went strong against it. Dr Barrow assured them that if they made a sorry building, they might fail of contributions; but if they made it very magnificent and stately, and, at least, exceeding that at Oxford, all gentlemen, of their interest, would generously contribute; it being what they desired, and little less than required of them; and money would not be wanted as the building went up, and occasion called for it. But sage caution prevailed, and the matter, at that time, was wholly laid aside. Dr Barrow was piqued at this pusillanimity, and declared that he would go straight to his college, and lay out the foundations of a building to enlarge his back court, and close it with a stately library, which should be more magnificent and costly than what he had proposed to them, and doubted not but upon the interest of his college, in a short time to bring it to perfection.[1] And he was as good as his word; for that very afternoon he, with his gardeners and servants, staked out the very foundation upon which the building now stands; and Dr North saw the finishing of it, except the classes [bookshelves], which were forward, but not done, in his time; and divers benefactions came in upon that account; wherewith, and the liberal supply from the college, the whole is rendered complete; and the admirable disposition and proportion on the inside is such as touches the very soul of any one who first sees it—

or of one who sees it for the hundredth time!

Two other buildings may be in part Wren's design—Bishop's Hostel and the rostrum in Nevile's Court. Bishop's Hostel is so called after John Hacket, Bishop of Lichfield and Coventry, who paid for its erection in place of the ruinous buildings of the older Garret Hostel. Willis and Clark (II, 555) write:

The entire building, which remains to this day with very slight alterations from its pristine form, was erected by Robert Minchin, of Blechington in the county of Oxford, carpenter,

[1] This story is quite consistent with other known facts, see Willis and Clark, III, 42–3. [Some doubts on this are expressed in P. Gaskell and R. Robson, *The Library of Trinity College, Cambridge: a short history* (Cambridge 1971), pp. 15–16.] The Senate House was eventually built in George I's reign.

in accordance with an agreement made between him and the Master and Fellows of the College, 15 January, 1669–70. This same individual was employed by Sir Christopher Wren in his works at Trinity College, Oxford, in 1665; and the design of the Bishop's Hostel is so much in Wren's manner that it may possibly have been revised by him. It is merely a stack of chambers, but is thrown into the form of a separate mansion, unconnected with the other buildings of the College.

In 1682, while the work on the Library was still unfinished, the College constructed the classical Rostrum, with three semicircular niches, stuck on to the west side of the Hall and looking down the length of Nevile's Court to the Library opposite. It is not improbable that it was designed by Wren (Willis and Clark, II, 550–1). The object was to harmonise the Tudor-Gothic of the Hall (probably already regarded by the taste of that day as 'barbarous') with the classical perfection of the Cloisters and the new Library. The steps up to the Hall screens from Nevile's Court were made at the same time.

A year or two before the Library was begun, the lime trees were planted that still form the avenue on the far side of the College bridge—'the long walk of limes' celebrated in the 87th poem of Tennyson's *In Memoriam*. Some half of them have now fallen and been replaced, but the veterans that remain are 270 years old (1942).* The limes on the east side of the river and the elms in the Fellows' garden to the west are of later date. In the seventeenth and eighteenth centuries the ground now occupied by the Fellows' garden was bare open cornfield.

After Barrow's untimely death in 1677 the College gradually deteriorated, though for another two decades Newton was doing his great work in our midst. The number of entries declined and the discipline of the undergraduates grew lax, partly because the standard of ability and conscientiousness among the Fellows was lowered by 'mandates' from the King, compelling the election of persons favoured by courtiers. The Revolution of 1688 put an end to this abuse, but it had been very bad during the previous decade, and its consequences

* [The lime avenue on the west side of the river was completely replanted in 1949.]

long survived in the inferior type of Fellow with whom Bentley had to deal in the reign of Anne. Charles II, though he would choose a good Master if left to himself, was not the man to resist the importunity of courtiers asking for the nomination of their favourites as Fellows of Trinity, over-riding the College's right of choice. Barrow's successor, North, struggled against this abuse by inducing the Seniority to make 'pre-elections' to Fellowships before they fell vacant, in itself an unsatisfactory device. But he complained that the Senior Fellows did not support him fully in the matter, and that some of them, behind his back, pushed their own favourites at Court.

John North, though the son of a peer, was very much the scholar and student. He was Greek Professor in the University, he was an early student of Descartes, and he had accumulated a vast mass of knowledge in many subjects, though constitutionally incapable of producing a book. In 1672 he had moved from Jesus where he held a Fellowship, to Trinity where he was content to be only a fellow-commoner, in order that he might enjoy the intellectual conversation of his friends Barrow and Newton. His residence at Trinity was a happy one, until in an evil hour his virtues and his learning were rewarded by the Mastership, a post of increasing difficulty for which he was by nature unfit. He was over-conscientious, fussy, and tactless, an excellent man but unable either to please or to govern young men or old, as is evident in many instances in the quaint biography that his brother wrote of him in *The Lives of the Norths*. He was a bachelor and an ascetic, who ruined his health by under-feeding and over-work. The beginning of the end came when he fell down in an epileptic fit while 'admonishing' two scholars who had misbehaved themselves: 'he was immediately taken up, and carried to his bed', writes his brother, 'wherein the two scholars were very assistant!' The barbarous pedantry of the medical profession of that day soon finished him off, though his mother for a while rescued him from their hands. The doctors had ordered him to be kept always awake by loud noises in his bedroom!

He died in 1683, and was buried in the ante-Chapel, in accordance with his own request 'that the Fellows might trample upon him dead, as they had done living'. The next Master laid to rest under that roof was Bentley in 1742, but he could hardly have said the same!

North was succeeded by the Hon. John Montagu, a younger son of the Earl of Sandwich, a man of the world whose unfitness for the Mastership was of a character quite different from the unfitness of his predecessor. Personally respectable, he was lax as an administrator through indifference and neglect, and the deterioration of discipline and learning went on apace. James II's mandates for elections to Fellowships were as bad as those of his brother, and met no resistance from Montagu. But during his Mastership the Library was completed with all its fittings, and the appearance of the College, thus perfected, was immortalised in Loggan's prints, published in the volume *Cantabrigia Illustrata* early in the reign of William III.

In Loggan's print of the Great Court, at the end of this book, it will be observed that the six grass plots, the cobbles and the paved pathways were situated much as now, but that the grass was surrounded by balustrades removed early in the following century. On the other hand, Nevile's Court had paths across the grass that have since been abolished.

In these prints of Trinity about the time of the Revolution, the accurate Loggan has depicted dogs in the Courts.[1] No objection was in those days felt to their presence, and indeed they were so ubiquitous in the College precincts that in 1665 'it was agreed that Dod have the place of keeping the dogs out of the Chapel'. In the following century, however, a very

[1] On the north side of the Great Court, a dog is barking at a large bird. This must represent the tame eagle, which we know from the College accounts was then kept and fed at the College expense. Loggan has represented a similar scene in his print of Lincoln College, Oxford. The Elizabethan Statutes of Trinity, which were in force till well on in the reign of Victoria, forbade (cap. xx) the *keeping* of dogs, ferrets or hawks in College, in the vain hope of discouraging undergraduates from addiction to field sports. But that is not the same thing as allowing dogs to stray into the Courts.

strong feeling against dogs in College grew up both at Oxford and Cambridge. And in the year 1806 Gillray, in the very amusing series of prints entitled *Rake's Progress at the University*, makes fun of the horror manifested at the sight of a dog in the Court:

> The Master's wig the guilty wight appals
> Who brings his dog within the College walls.

So strict by that time was the rule that Lort Mansel, when Master of Trinity and Bishop of Bristol, was obliged to carry his dog 'Isaac' in his arms whenever he crossed the Court going to or from the Lodge (Gunning, *Reminiscences*, II, 118).*

The attempt made under Elizabeth and James I to saddle Trinity with an inordinate number of old Westminsters as scholars of Trinity and subsequently as Fellows, had been strongly resisted by the College. After much controversy it had been agreed as a compromise that three scholars a year must be taken from Westminster, but that none of them should have an extraordinary right to a Fellowship. It became, however, the custom to elect the senior Westminster bachelor scholar into a Fellowship. Consequently, between 1600 and 1700 very nearly half the Fellows of Trinity were old Westminsters. The excellence of the school under Busby partly accounts for this very high proportion, but even so it was an abuse. Between 1701 and 1775 the proportion of old Westminsters among the Fellows was rather less—about one-third. After 1775 the preference for Westminsters as Fellows came suddenly to an end, and between 1800 and 1856 only four Westminster scholars obtained Fellowships.[1]

* [It is not certain that Gunning meant to imply that Mansel carried Isaac as Master. A comparison of p. 118 with p. 111, where Gunning records meeting Mansel and Isaac in 1784, perhaps suggests that Gunning is referring to the period when Mansel was still a Fellow; he did not become Master until 1798.

Dogs have appeared in College on later occasions. In 1845 Whewell as Master rebuked the Vice-Master, Adam Sedgwick, for taking his dog into the College Courts. (J. W. Clark and T. M. Hughes, *The Life and Letters of the Reverend Adam Sedgwick* (Cambridge, 1890), vol. II, p. 98.]

[1] See McLeod Innes, *Fellows of Trinity College*, 1941, pp. 13-14 and Winstanley's *Unreformed Cambridge*, pp. 231-2.

The names of the Westminster scholars will be found in the volume published by Joseph Welch in 1788. During the Stuart period they do not seem to me to include as many eminent names as one might expect, though we owe to the close Westminster scholarships the right of claiming as Trinity men the poets George Herbert and John Dryden. Charles Montagu, Earl of Halifax, and Judge Jeffreys were both of them at Westminster and at Trinity, but neither of them came here as Westminster scholars. Jeffreys only stayed one year (1662) and did not take a degree; nothing is recorded of him as a Trinity man, and Macaulay has nothing to say about that part of his career! Charles Montagu, on the other hand, made the most of College life, became a Fellow, and learnt by his friendship with Newton much that helped him to become England's great financier.

CHAPTER VI

BENTLEY 1700–1742

DURING the first four decades of the eighteenth century the history of our College can be summed up in one word—Bentley. But that word involves many matters.

Towards the end of 1699 Montagu resigned the Mastership on his appointment to the Deanery of Durham. Who was to succeed him?

In those days the ecclesiastical patronage of the Crown, of which the Mastership of Trinity was regarded as part, was not dispensed by the Prime Minister but by the monarch in person. The patronage had been exercised by the good Anglican Queen Mary II until her death in 1694. After that, her husband, William III, as a Dutchman and a latitudinarian Calvinist, felt it prudent to leave Church patronage to a Commission of Bishops; when Montagu left Trinity, the Commission consisted of Archbishops Tenison and Sharp, Bishops Lloyd, Burnet, Patrick and Moore. These learned and capable men made a choice for which they cannot be blamed, whether or not it is to be regretted. They knew that the College had been going down hill for some years, and to restore its discipline and learning they looked round for a strong administrator and great scholar. Such a man they rightly saw in Richard Bentley, who had just triumphed over the fine wit and inferior scholarship of Christ Church in the famous Phalaris controversy. His *Dissertation upon the Epistles of Phalaris* is not only the greatest controversial work of pure learning that has ever been written, but it began a new era in the study of classical antiquities, chronology and philology. Never before or since has so much learning been used for so many purposes with such skill.[1]

[1] A. E. Housman, 'Shropshire Lad' and classical scholar, spent the last years of his life (1911–36) as Fellow of Trinity. I have been told

It is to the credit of the board of Bishops that they realised the merits of the book within a few months of its publication, for Oxford and the world of fashion had not yet admitted the completeness of Bentley's victory and achievement. The Bishops were also right in their belief that Bentley had unusual ability as an administrator and that he was an utterly fearless man. Here, they thought, was the ideal reformer of the College. It was scarcely their fault if they failed to suspect his latent tyranny and arrogance, for those features of his character had not yet displayed themselves on any public stage. Throughout the Phalaris controversy he had observed a prudence and care which he never condescended to employ in the composition of his subsequent works. The arrogance indeed had all been on the side of the light-weights of Christ Church.

Bentley was at the time King's Librarian, not resident at Cambridge. But he had been bred a Johnian. When he was appointed to Trinity he is said to have exclaimed, 'With the help of my God I have leaped over a wall'—referring to the high wall that still divides our Bowling Green from the John's Lane.

For forty years to come he kept not only the College but the University simmering and exploding with angry broils, punctuated by rival pamphlets and involving a ceaseless succession of lawsuits, an element which he enjoyed as a fish the water, or rather as a salamander enjoys the fire. His ability was consummate. Usually in the wrong, he usually had the best of it, and even when defeated for a while he always rose again triumphant. His long story is like the old drama of Punch, who knocks down one adversary after another, save that *our* Punch never met his match even at the end.

The story of this Forty Years' War is long and highly complicated, but it has been recorded fully, delightfully and impartially in the two volumes of James Monk's *Life of Bentley*

his opinion of the other great Trinity classics: he would submit to be compared to Porson, not to mention Jebb, but grew angry if anyone attempted to put him or anyone else in the same class as Bentley the great.

(1830), one of the best biographies in the language. By reading that book it is possible to know more about Trinity during that unhappy time than during any other period before the Mastership of Whewell. Monk had every qualification for his task. He had been Greek Professor at Cambridge and Tutor of Trinity,[1] and he had at his service the College records and the voluminous papers of Bentley and of his enemies.

Under the Statutes of the College, power was divided between the Master and the Seniority, that is the eight Senior Fellows, an oligarchy not chosen by, or necessarily representing, the fifty other Fellows. Bentley had a largely justified contempt for the Seniors, which unfortunately led him to treat them very ill, either dispensing with their consent to his actions, or rudely demanding it. A state of feeling was soon engendered, rendering it difficult to carry on the business of the College without chicanery and violence to the Statutes, which presupposed a certain degree of concurrence between the Master and the Seniors. It must indeed be remembered that the Elizabethan Statutes had never been revised, were largely out of date, and had by custom been long disregarded in many particulars by all parties. But Bentley, besides breaking any of the Statutes which he found inconvenient, on other occasions revived their most obsolete parts in order to penalise opposition—calling them 'his rusty sword'.

The new Master had indeed a much better idea than the Seniority of what a College ought to be. He was not only England's supreme classical scholar of all time; he also had ideas far beyond the general academic purview of his age, of making this University, and above all this College, the seat of high studies in all other great subjects, particularly in the Physical Sciences. He was in personal correspondence with the most learned men on the Continent of Europe, and brought

[1] Macaulay, in his private journal now in the Trinity Library, notes in 1852 when he met his old Tutor, Monk, again, as Bishop of Gloucester, 'He was kind to me when I was young and I was ungrateful and impertinent to him.' There is a good short life of Bentley by Jebb.

over some of them, such as Sike of Bremen, the Orientalist, to be members of our College. If he had not been an arrogant and self-interested tyrant, he would have succeeded even more fully in these his nobler ambitions.

Even as he was, he did great things for Science. His biographer Monk, who lived a hundred years nearer those times than we do, has testified that it was very largely due to Bentley that Cambridge, and above all Trinity, became the seat of Newtonian studies and philosophy.

Newton and Bentley were friends. From the first each recognised the other's greatness. And their friendship was never broken, because Newton went away from Trinity to London in 1696, four years before Bentley became Master. If he had remained among us, a man so severely just as Newton would not have fallen in with Bentley's malpractices. In London, as Master of the Mint, he was not called upon to take sides in the disputes of his old College, and he was too prudent a man to jump into the mud when it was not his duty to wade through it.

The friendship of the two great men was therefore unbroken, and Bentley continued all his life to give full scope to his Newtonian enthusiasm. He made himself the effective patron of Newton's young followers, especially of Roger Cotes and Robert Smith, whom he closely attached to the College. He did much to promote the second edition of Newton's *Principia* which Cotes so ably edited; and when the young man became the first Plumian Professor of Astronomy, Bentley erected for him an observatory on the top of the Great Gate. It was then the only observatory in Cambridge. Its cupola disfigured the beauty of the Gate until its removal in 1797.[1] (See print, p. 55.)

Premature death deprived the world of Cotes, of whom Newton said, 'Had he lived, we might have known something' (1716). But Bentley's other Newtonian protégé, Robert Smith, lived to become Master of the College, healed the Bentleian

[1] In 1708 Newton presented to the College the huge grandfather clock now in the entrance hall of the Lodge. It is said that it was originally used in the observatory.

feuds, and founded for the University the famous Smith's Prizes. A striking portrait of him hangs in the Hall.

Besides the observatory, Bentley also established a chemical laboratory in the mediaeval chambers that look out on the Bowling Green. This action was rendered suspect to the Fellows, by the fact that the Master was at that time trying to steal their Bowling Green to add to his garden; as also to deprive them of the Combination Room, where, as he said, they hatched treason against him.

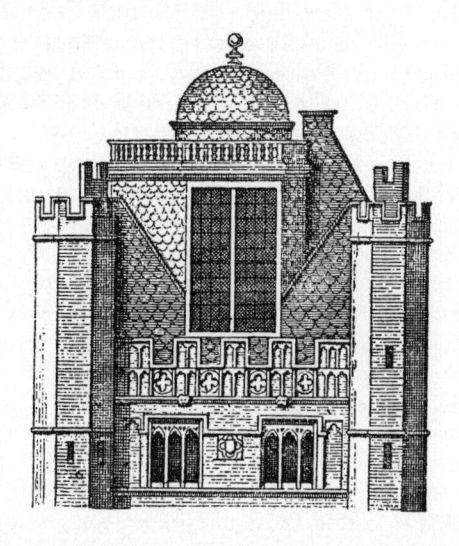

Bentley's genuine desire for the progress of learning in all its branches was largely stultified by another motive in his College policy. He was avaricious, autocratic and self-interested to a degree, and regarded the Mastership as a means of obtaining money and power for himself, often in unstatutable and even dishonest ways. In most of these designs he succeeded, although the Fellows managed to save their beloved Bowling Green. His greed and love of rule so far swallowed up his zeal as a reformer that he caused his son to be elected a Fellow at the age of fifteen. Nor was this the worst of the elections he countenanced for personal reasons. The impartial reward of merit among the members of the College was incompatible with the Master's system of refusing scholarships and Fellowships to the pupils of those Tutors who sided against him.

Trinity was for forty years divided between a Bentleian and an anti-Bentleian party; even the undergraduates found their own fortunes involved in the divisions of their elders. The anti-Bentleian party was at first much the larger, but as death removed the older men, and the Master's forceful intrigues replaced them with his own partisans, the balance was gradually tilted the other way. To resist him seemed at length hopeless to all save the most gallant spirits, like Colbatch, who fought the battle to the end from his retreat in the rectory of Orwell.

The higher academic talent of the College was not unequally divided between the two parties. The young Newtonians, Cotes and Smith, stood by their patron; while the classical scholar and latitudinarian divine Conyers Middleton employed his clear and caustic style in pamphlets against Bentley, as well as in founding the modern school of scepticism about miracles in the age of the Fathers.

The College suffered so much from the greatest of its Masters that it has scarcely yet forgiven him. His portrait does not hang in the Hall*, still less in the Combination Room. And when, in 1856, it was decided to place a third statue in the ante-Chapel beside those of Newton and Bacon, Barrow was chosen and Bentley rejected.[1]

---

* [A full-length portrait of Bentley hung in the Hall above the panelling until the 1920's.]

[1] Macaulay detested Bentley's insolence and injustice, as is clearly shown by his marginal notes made in the copy of Monk's *Bentley* which I possess. [Macaulay's copy of Monk's Life of Bentley is now in the College Library.] None the less, Macaulay, alone of those consulted by Whewell in the matter, was in favour of a statue to Bentley, and gave his reasons as follows: 'In the studies from which Bentley derives his fame, we are, I believe, unrivalled. And this is to be attributed partly to the influence of his genius. To this day, unless I deceive myself, the scholarship of Trinity men has a peculiar character which may be called Bentleian, and which is not found in the scholarship of men who have gained the highest honors of

There is however one part of the College where his memory is cultivated, and where the portraits of himself, his wife and his friends are prominent on the walls. The inhabitants of the Master's Lodge which he embellished must needs be grateful to him, and look with a lenient eye at the questionable methods by which that embellishment was effected.

Between 1700 and 1709, the years during which Marlborough was winning his famous victories, the Lodge was transformed from a mainly Tudor to a mainly Queen Anne mansion. The finest features of Nevile's decoration, the ceiling and fireplace of the large drawing-room, were fortunately not destroyed, although the ceiling (regarded, I suppose, as 'Gothic') was hidden by a flat ceiling introduced below it, and so survived unseen, to delight the more catholic taste of later times when its original beauty was uncovered once more. Bentley also replaced the Elizabethan windows of the Lodge with large sash windows, except in the oriels which he left untouched (see p. 58, print *circa* 1740). The anti-Bentleian Fellows justly complained that the new sash windows 'broke the Uniformity of the Quadrangle', and more than a century later Whewell replaced them with the older type, in harmony with the rest of the Great Court. But he left those of Bentley's sash windows that still look out on the Master's garden from the state bedrooms.

Having read thus far, the reader may exclaim that Bentley did more harm than good to the Lodge. But this was not all. His grand staircase, and his panelling of the dining-room and the state bedrooms of the Judges' and the King's suites are in the very best style of Queen Anne decoration, and give the Lodge half its dignity. The high panelling of the period can nowhere be seen in greater perfection, and since the College

Oxford. I am far from putting Bentley in the same rank with Newton. But in one respect the two men may fairly be classed together. They were the two intellectual founders of our college. Their minds have left an impress which is still plainly discernible. They may, therefore, with peculiar propriety, appear together in our antechapel.' Winstanley, *Early Victorian Cambridge*, pp. 436–9.

authorities in 1941 stripped the paint off the oak wainscot of the dining-room, that room is very pleasant to the eye.[1]

But these changes in the Lodge were not made without the most dreadful quarrels. When Bentley first came to Trinity, the Seniors, who did not yet know with what manner of man they had to deal, gratified the new Master by signing him a blank cheque in the following terms:

Ordered then by the Master and Seniors, that the Master's Lodge be repaird and finishd with new Seeling, Wainscot, Flooring and other convenient improvements; towards which Expense the Master will contribute *de proprio* the Summ of one hundred pounds sterling.[2]

The Seniors afterwards alleged that Bentley had obtained this order from them by promising that the whole work on the Lodge would not cost more than £300—which he denied. Be that as it may, he had soon spent £1600 without consulting anyone as to the panelling, the sash windows, the new marble

[1] See note at end of chapter on the panelling of the Lodge.
[2] This is dated April 11, 1700. In the Conclusion Book it bears the signatures of Bentley and all eight Seniors.

fireplaces, or anything else. The Seniors considered that they had been choused of over £1000 of College revenue.

But worse was yet to come. Bentley suddenly determined that there must be a new staircase of the spacious eighteenth-century type, to match the modern style of windows and panelling which he had introduced into the rooms. The little old Tudor staircase presumably stood in the entrance hall. Bentley pulled it down and built out a new brick shell on the west side of the entrance hall, to contain the present grand staircase which he proceeded to build. The Fellows refused to pay for it, and the Bursar came to bid the workmen desist. The Master appeared on the scene, angrily bade the workmen proceed and shouted at the Bursar, 'I will send you into the country to feed my turkeys'. The staircase was finished, and Bentley found ways of penalising the Fellows till they agreed to pay for it. But one of the charges made against the Master before the judgment seat of the Visitor ran as follows:

Why did you of your own Head pull down a good Stair-case in your Lodge, and give Orders and Directions for building a new one, and that too fine for common Use?

The sympathies of posterity must needs be divided. It is equally impossible to approve Bentley's methods, or to regret the panelling of the rooms and the making of the staircase 'too fine for common Use'.

Bentley's own defence of his improvements, not only in the Lodge ('Master's Apartment') but elsewhere in the College, was put forward to the Visitor in 1710 in the following flamboyant and provocative terms:

It has been often told me by Persons of Sense and Candour, that when I left them I might say of the College, what *Augustus* said of *Rome*, *Lateritium inveni, marmoreum reliqui*. The College-Chappel, from a decay'd antiquated Model, made one of the noblest in *England*; the College-Hall, from a dirty, sooty Place, restor'd to its Original Beauty, and excel'd by none in Cleanliness and Magnificence. The Master's Apartment (if that may be nam'd without Envy) from a spacious Jail, from want of room in an excess of it, made worthy of that Royal Foundation, and of the Guests it's sometimes honour'd with: An elegant

Chymical Laboratory, where Courses are annually taught by a Professor, made out of a ruinous Lumber-Hole, the thieving House of the Bursars of the old Set, who in spite of frequent Orders to prevent it, would still embezzle there the College-Timber: the College-Gatehouse rais'd up and improved to a stately Astronomical Observatory, well stor'd with the best Instruments in Europe. In a word, every Garret of the House well repair'd and inhabited, many of which were wast and empty before my coming. (Willis and Clark, II, 616.)

The reference Bentley here makes to the improvements then begun in the College Chapel reminds us that to this period we owe the woodwork of the stalls, organ and the baldachino over the altar. [The organ, which had been enlarged in the nineteenth century, has now (1976) been restored to its original appearance and character.] About this also there were the usual quarrels between the Master and some of the Fellows, although both sides showed an admirable liberality in the matter of the Chapel, the Fellows with very few exceptions subscribing the amount of their own annual dividend, and even Bentley producing £200. During his too brief lifetime, the astronomer Cotes collected the subscriptions and supervised the work, though it was not finished when he died in 1716.

The interest taken by Cotes in the Chapel is characteristic of this epoch in our College history, when the men of science from Newton downwards were no less religious, and were perhaps more truly 'Christian', than the quarrelsome Doctors of Divinity. When a generation later Roubiliac's statue of Newton was set up in the ante-Chapel, it fitly symbolised the harmony between religion and science in which the English of that latitudinarian age securely believed. The Creator was to be seen and worshipped by the study of his creation. Cotes as Professor of Astronomy must have warmly approved the words written by Addison in 1712:

> The spacious firmament on high,
> With all the blue ethereal sky,
> And spangled Heavens, a shining frame,
> Their great Original proclaim.

In 1726 the present clock and dial plate were put up on the Edward III Tower. Thenceforward the double chime at the hour has been heard by Trinity men, and by their nearest neighbours on the other side of John's Lane, such as the young William Wordsworth, who, in the years immediately preceding the French Revolution, used to listen in his rooms to

> Trinity's loquacious clock,
> Who never let the quarters, night or day
> Slip by him unproclaimed, and told the hours
> Twice over with a male and female voice.
> (*Prelude*, III, 53–56.)

In Bentley's day three successive sovereigns visited Cambridge, and more particularly Trinity, not staying for the night but coming over for the day from their holiday headquarters at Newmarket. In 1705 Queen Anne paid such a visit, dined in state in our Hall, and knighted Sir Isaac Newton in the Lodge. At a visit of George I twelve years later a distressing mistake was made. Bentley and the whole College were very naturally waiting at the Great Gate to receive the royal party, who were known to be attending service in King's Chapel. But the Vice-Chancellor, in order to show his own College of Clare, brought them by the back way and tried to enter by the Queen's Gate, which was barred as no notice had been given. There the King stood in the mud of Trinity Lane for five minutes, till word at last got round to the loyal assembly at the Great Gate, who thereupon hurried across the Court to let him in. He dined privately in the Lodge with twelve noblemen, while the Chancellor, 'the proud Duke of Somerset', who had sent his son to Trinity, presided over a state banquet in the Hall. In 1728 a similar visit from Newmarket was paid by George II, attended by 'seven dukes'! He dined 'seated in an elevated chair of state at the upper end of the Hall, and waited on by twelve Fellow-commoners of the College; Dr Bentley standing by his side and remaining in conversation with him while at dinner'.

Before leaving the subject of Bentley, we must briefly describe his two citations before the Court of the Bishop of Ely as Visitor of the College, in 1710–14 and 1728–34 respectively, when twice over he escaped in the strangest manner and by the narrowest possible margin from paying the full penalty of his misdeeds.

On both occasions his accusers were a party of the Fellows, bringing against him a long list of charges of breach of Statutes and malversation of College property. On both occasions he was able to protract the proceedings for several years, partly by political influence, and partly by disputing the right of the Bishop of Ely to act as Visitor of the College. The Tudor Statutes had in fact left a real uncertainty whether the Crown or the Bishop was the Visitor. Bentley's contention that the power lay with the Crown was not unreasonable, and has in fact since his day prevailed. It was naturally not unwelcome to Government and to the royal judges.

In those days politics lay behind everything, to a greater or less extent. Bentley trimmed his political course very shrewdly, but not, I think, dishonestly. His real principles were more Whig than Tory, but he was not a party man. Early in Queen Anne's reign he stood by her Marlborough-Godolphin War Ministry and its Whig supporters. During the Tory reaction of 1710–14, like many other moderates, he rallied to the moderate Harley and welcomed the Peace of Utrecht. On Queen Anne's death he came out as an uncompromising advocate of the Hanoverian succession, nor is there any doubt that his anti-Jacobite zeal was life-long and sincere. At no moment, therefore, was he in very bad odour with the Government of the day, and after 1714 his enemies were under the disadvantage of their High Church and Tory connections.

The King's Courts again and again showed favour to Bentley. They treated his adversaries Colbatch and Conyers Middleton with great harshness in several suits in which they became involved, and in 1724 compelled the University to restore Bentley to all his degrees. He had been deprived of them six years before by a vote of the Senate, in consequence of his violent quarrel with the Vice-Chancellor, in the course of which his servants at Trinity Lodge had locked the Esquire Bedell into the dining-room for two hours!

Just as in the end he triumphed over the University, so in the end he triumphed over the College. In his first trial before Moore, Bishop of Ely, the Bishop in 1714 had actually drawn up the sentence of condemnation depriving him of his Mastership—but suddenly died before he was able to read the judgment in Court![1]

After being saved by that extraordinary accident, Bentley went on as before, and the next Bishop of Ely, Fleetwood, refused to act as judge in his case. At length Fleetwood was succeeded by Green, and in 1728 the undying zeal of the Master's enemies began yet another assault upon him in the new Bishop's Court. The adversaries on both sides were now aged men, but Bentley's vigour and astuteness were in no wise abated. By appeals to the Government and to the lay courts the Master protracted the case till 1734, when he was over seventy years old; then at last it seemed that there was an end of his shifts, and the Bishop of Ely pronounced sentence against him. He was condemned to be deprived of the Mastership.

That would have been the end of any one save Bentley. But he found a last line of defence. By the Elizabethan Statutes the sentence of the Visitor ordering the Master's deprivation was to be carried out by the Vice-Master; the existing Vice-Master, Hacket, who only wished to make himself safe, gladly

[1] Bishop Moore had collected a magnificent library, which on his death George I bought for £6000 and presented to the University, eliciting the famous Oxford epigram:

> The King observing with judicious eyes,
> The state of both his universities,
> To one he sends a regiment; For why?
> That learned body wanted loyalty.
> To th'other books he sent, as well discerning
> How much the loyal body wanted learning.

and the Cambridge reply:

> The King to Oxford sent a troop of horse;
> For Tories own no argument but force.
> With equal care, to Cambridge books he sent;
> For Whigs allow no force but argument.

resigned the dangerous post, and Bentley at once secured the election in his place of his own faithful friend Richard Walker.[1] The new Vice-Master refused to act, and Bentley remained in the Lodge, enjoying the revenues and exercising the functions of Master. His accusers, thus deprived of the fruits of their victory, spent four more years moving the King's Courts for a *mandamus* to compel the Vice-Master to do his duty and expel his friend from the position he had forfeited. But all was in vain, and the old badger lay snug in his earth, undrawn. The death of Bishop Green in 1738 at length put an end to the long contest, and Bentley spent the last four years of his life unassailed. But such was the old man's warlike temper to the end, that he still continued to harass his enemies with lawsuits.

He made the College pay all the legal expenses of his defence which amounted to four thousand pounds.

The Vice-Master, Walker, who thus saved his aged friend by bold inaction, earned a place in English literature beside Bentley in the Fourth Book of Pope's *Dunciad*, published in 1742, a few months before the Master's death:

> Where Bentley late tempestuous wont to sport
> In troubled waters, but now sleeps in port.
> Before them march'd that awful Aristarch;
> Ploughed was his front with many a deep remark:
> His hat, which never vail'd to human pride,
> Walker with reverence took, and laid aside.

Then follows Bentley's speech, ending

> 'Walker! our hat', nor more he deigned to say,
> But stern as Ajax' spectre, strode away.

---

[1] In the Conclusion Book for May 17, 1734, about three weeks after the Visitor's sentence had been pronounced, we read Hacket's resignation, and then the following entry: 'The Master and Seniors accepted the Resignation of the late Vicemaster, and appointed Richard Walker D.D. to be Vicemaster for the remaining part of the year. Ri: Bentley.'

Walker, as his portrait in the Lodge suggests, was a cheerful, good-natured, sensible person; instead of taking these lines in dudgeon, after the Master's death he hung up the famous hat on a peg in his rooms, and used to show it laughingly to his friends. It was an enormous three-cornered head-shield which Bentley in his last years wore to protect his eyes.[1]

Bentley's family life and his personal friendships were in striking contrast to the hard front he presented to his enemies. His wife, whom he made very happy, was a clever and charming woman, who managed to be popular even with the party in the College opposed to her husband. Their younger daughter, Joanna, called 'Jug' Bentley by her father and by the world, was a beautiful and sprightly girl. At the age of eleven she was celebrated in the *Spectator* for Oct. 6, 1714, in the playful verses beginning:

> My Time, O ye Muses, was happily spent,
> When Phoebe went with me wherever I went.

The author was a young Fellow of Trinity, John Byrom, who, though his works are included in editions of our English poets, never again wrote anything as good.*

Bentley's conversation with his intimates must have been highly entertaining, though sometimes formidable. His caustic wit is known to posterity in the Preface to the *Dissertation* on Phalaris, and a few fragments of his lost conversations have drifted down the tide of time. There is his damaging verdict on claret, 'It would be port if it could' (Monk's *Life*, II, 401); and his brutal answer to the Master of another College who, at the end of a long discussion, observed, 'It is not yet quite clear to me', when Bentley replied, 'Are we then to wait till your mud has subsided?' (Monk, II, 48).

The Lodge owes to him a number of its most interesting pictures. In 1710 he employed Thornhill to paint the well-

---

[1] Walker was a benefactor of the University. In 1762 he founded the Botanical Garden, buying land for its institution and endowment. He expressly stated that it was to carry on the work of Ray (see p. 38 above).

* [Byrom also wrote the hymn 'Christians Awake' in 1749.]

known portraits of himself and his wife, and the most life-like of the many portraits of Newton (see p. 42 above). He also left to the Lodge the enormous picture by the same artist of Baron Ezekiel Spanheim, the Prussian scholar and diplomat of an older generation, who had befriended him in the Phalaris days. He has also left us a small picture of Scaliger, the Huguenot of a century before, who alone of modern men approached his eminence as a classical scholar.

One of the most damaging charges made in the Visitor's Court against the Master had been that in defiance of the Statutes he constantly absented himself from Chapel. He had written against the Free-thinkers with force and effect, but he was very impatient of being bored. On one occasion when he had deigned to attend service, he could not get into the Master's stall, because after long disuse the door had been fastened up! His name and arms are carved over that stall, and his friend Walker's over the stall of the Vice-Master.

But Bentley came to Chapel in the end. In July 1742 he died at the age of eighty, and was buried on the north side of the communion rails. There the flat stone that covers him may still be found, inscribed with academic titles that do not include that of Master of the College, because he was still under the sentence of deprivation passed on him eight years before his death.* But if ever man was Master of Trinity, it was he.

Now that two hundred years have passed, we may say of him what Andrew Fairservice said of another robber chief: 'There are many things ower bad for praising, and ower good for banning—like Rob Roy.' His fame is ours. And in the world of creative scholarship that fame stands higher than that of any other Trinity man—except immortal Newton.

* [Bentley's grave stone was paid for by his family, who presumably acquiesced in the omission in the inscription.]

NOTE ON THE PANELLING OF
THE LODGE, ETC.

Some at least of the panels in the entrance hall are Tudor or early Stuart and the rest are in imitation of that style. These small panels of the older style contrast with the large Queen Anne panels in the dining-room next door and in the state bedrooms beyond.

It is possible, though not certain, that in order to get room for his high panels and high sash windows, Bentley raised the level of the Judges' state bedrooms and the King's rooms above; so at least one might surmise from the blocked-up older windows on a different level which are visible from the Master's garden. In that west wall of the Lodge facing the garden, the white clunch stone dates from Nevile's original building and the bricks from Bentley's alterations. Possibly a lot of the clunch needed renewing even in his day. A great deal of it had to be replaced in 1941.

Inside the Lodge, Bentley's large Queen Anne panelling replaced old worn-out tapestry, wall-painting and possibly some Tudor panels. The state bedrooms certainly owe their present panels to Bentley. And the dining-room was panelled either by him or by one of his near predecessors. I think it was by Bentley himself, and that Willis and Clark (*Arch. Hist. of Cam.* II, 610 and note) are wrong in supposing that Bentley found the dining-room already 'wainscoted with oak'. The reason they give for so thinking is Monk's brief note (*Life*, I, 149–50, ed. 1833), 'Only the dining-room was wainscoted with oak'. But that expression, I think, means that the dining-room was the only room to which Bentley gave wainscot of oak instead of the inferior woods (painted no doubt) which he used to panel the state bedrooms beyond.

Early in 1941 the dining-room panels, much in need of mending, were taken down and repaired, and the paint was removed from them to expose the bare oak. This operation revealed that there were six coats of paint on them, the lowest and oldest being white. The skilled workmen employed were of opinion that the panels had originally been set up in some other place and brought thence to their present position, but whether this was so or not it proves nothing as to the date of their erection in the dining-room. That date, I have little doubt, was the early years of Bentley's Mastership.

When stripped of paint in 1941, nearly a quarter of the dining-room panels and mouldings proved to be deal, irregularly distributed, but largely at the north end of the room. The deal was replaced by oak to harmonise with the rest (1941). Possibly the large proportion of deal was due to the fact that the dining-room was, after Bentley's day, shortened at its north end to make room for the passage leading into the garden from the Judges' suite. The north side of that passage still has the panels which originally decorated the north end of the dining-room, so that when the passage was made, more panels had somehow to be procured for the new north end of the shortened dining-room, and possibly it was then that so much deal came to be employed.

CHAPTER VII

THE LATER EIGHTEENTH CENTURY

MASTERS OF TRINITY

1742: ROBERT SMITH
1768: JOHN HINCHLIFFE (Bishop of Peterborough)
1789: THOMAS POSTLETHWAITE
1798–1820: WILLIAM LORT MANSEL (Bishop of Bristol)

THE LAST sixty years of the eighteenth century, or in terms of classical scholarship the period between Bentley and Porson, form a time of relative stagnation in Trinity, as in other Colleges both here and at Oxford. But before considering the life of the College during this backwater of its history, let us first note the changes that then took place in its outward appearance, and the chief additions that were made to its artistic treasures.

Robert Smith, the Newtonian Master who healed the feuds that his predecessor had caused in our society, was not inactive in the care of the College fabric. The poor material of much of Nevile's stonework (see p. 26 above) rendered necessary very extensive repairs. Between 1750 and 1754 the whole south side of the Great Court, including the Queen's Gate, was refaced with better stone, and long stretches of the other sides were covered with stucco, always excepting the well-built fifteenth-century clock tower (Willis and Clark, II, 495). Since then, various other parts of the Court have been refaced with stone; some of it in our own day has been taken from the quarries at Ketton which Wren used for the Library.

Similarly, Nevile's Court itself required attention. The Cloisters were decaying, because the spandrels of the arches and other parts of the front walls had been built of chalky, local clunch that easily crumbled away. They were therefore rebuilt in better stone in 1755–6. The fashionable architect

THE LATER EIGHTEENTH CENTURY

Essex, in accordance with the taste of the day, took the occasion to remove some Jacobean ornament from the face of the walls, and to abolish the gables above the upper windows, in favour of the present balustrade, similar to that which Wren had placed along the top of the neighbouring Library.

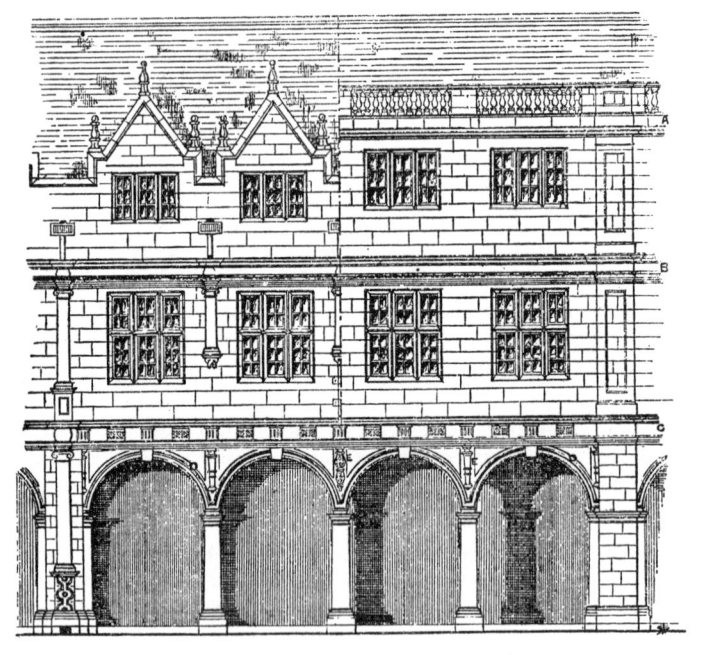

Cloisters before 1756   Cloisters after 1756

During the same decade certain members of the College had the happy idea of engaging the services of the sculptor Roubiliac, to adorn the Library with historical busts of former Trinity men. The most beautiful are those of Ray and Willughby at the two sides of the entrance door (see p. 38 above), but all are good. The Victorian busts of later Trinity worthies which now complete the series are, I fear, much less good, with the possible exception of Woolner's bust of the young, still beardless, Tennyson.*

Roubiliac's work at Trinity was crowned by his statue of Newton, which the Master presented to the ante-Chapel. It is the finest work of art in the College, as well as the most moving and significant. The lips parted and the eyes turned up in thought give life to marble. The inscription, *Qui genus humanum ingenio superavit*, is a pun ennobled by its truth.[1]

A generation later, a young Johnian undergraduate, William Wordsworth, lived in rooms just across the lane that divides the two Colleges, commanding a view of our ante-Chapel:

> And from my pillow, looking forth by light
> Of Moon or favouring stars, I could behold
> The antechapel where the statue stood
> Of Newton with his prism and silent face,
> The marble index of a mind for ever
> Voyaging through strange seas of thought, alone.
> (*Prelude*, III, 58–63.)

A large proportion of our College plate dates from the eighteenth century. Anyone who examines the pieces will usually find an inscription recording presentation by a nobleman or fellow-commoner, with his arms and those of the College. I used to think it remarkable and rather touching that these high-spirited young gentlemen, often not very amenable to discipline or much addicted to study, should have so regularly been at the trouble, to say nothing of the expense, of making these delightful presents to their College. But in fact the affair stood on a less romantic basis. Mr Winstanley has now explained to us (*Unreformed Cambridge*, p. 200) that there was a rule that every nobleman should give plate to the value of twenty pounds and every fellow-commoner to the value of fifteen, and that in 1727 the Seniority made their Tutors

---

[1] The Master, Robert Smith, also presented to the Library a bust by Scheemakers of his long-lost friend and competitor Cotes; but it has not the quality of the busts by Roubiliac.

* [The nineteenth-century busts have now been placed elsewhere in the College; that of Tennyson is in the Lower Library. The eighteenth-century busts remain in the Library.]

responsible for seeing that it was done. The aristocratic donor, so long as he was in residence, used his gift of plate at the Fellows' table where he dined, and left it behind him when he went down. In 1752 a nobleman's contribution was raised to twenty-five pounds, and the cash was to be placed with the Junior Bursar as caution money on admission, till the plate materialised.

It was an excellent arrangement, by the results of which later generations greatly benefit, for in those days it was easy to obtain for twenty-five pounds, or even fifteen, pieces which we now very much admire. We have still plenty of these 'benevolences' left to adorn our board, but a good deal of the Trinity plate was stolen in 1798 by Kidman, the ingenious robber of so many Cambridge Colleges, whose remarkable life story has been fully told by Gunning (*Reminiscences of Cambridge*, II, 103, 125–31, 269–73).

During the Mastership of Hinchliffe, nearly twenty-five years after the changes effected in the Cloisters, Essex was again let loose, this time on the Great Court, which it was thought necessary to 'touch with the hand of taste'. Between 1770 and 1775 the south end of the west side of the Court, then containing the Combination Room as well as the Kitchens, was 'degothicised', the trefoil oriel was removed, and the whole range refaced in the simple, classical elegance that it presents to-day. At that time the Lodge displayed Bentley's sash windows, which harmonised with these improvements on the other side of the Hall. Why not finish the good work? The idea was entertained of engaging Essex to rebuild the whole Great Court in the same style! Fortunately financial considerations acted as a brake on the rage for improvement, and nothing more was done, except that a few years later the lovely semi-circular oriel of the Lodge was removed.[1]

[1] I say 'a few years later' than 1775 because there is in the Lodge an old print of that period which shows the Court as it was *after* Essex's operations with the Kitchen wing, but with the Lodge oriel still extant. Soon after this it was gone. It is often said that Bentley removed it, but in fact he did not.

With the coming of the Gothic revival in the nineteenth century, the tide of fashion swung back, and Whewell in 1842 restored the Elizabethan windows to the front of the Lodge, and rebuilt its oriel, not however in the old semi-circular form but as a polygon, with a new Gothic gable above, as can still be seen. After the War of 1914–18 it was proposed, in a similar spirit, to spend a large sum of money, already collected for a War Memorial to Trinity men, in undoing the work of Essex in the Kitchen corner and restoring the trefoil oriel. After long vacillation and debate it was decided to leave the work of Essex alone, as a 'period piece' that had already for 150 years been part of the College life.

To the taste of 1775 we also owe the coloured window at the south end of the Library, representing fame introducing Newton to George III, while Bacon sits by, taking a note of the proceedings. Britannia whispers into the monarch's ear, coaching him perhaps, 'Sir Isaac Newton, the famous scientist, you know, Sir!'

During the first ninety years of the eighteenth century, Trinity was unworthy of its past and of its future. The numbers of undergraduates went down to about half of what they had been in Tudor and Stuart times, though the decline had begun in the middle of Charles II's reign (see A Note on Numbers at the end of the chapter). This decline in numbers was no less observable in the aggregate of other Oxford and Cambridge Colleges, although until the last years of the century Trinity had fewer undergraduates and fewer academic successes than John's.

The fall in numbers was a well-deserved punishment for corruption and incompetence. The public in early Hanoverian times ceased to value English University education, which could only be had at Oxford or Cambridge, and which like other monopoly articles was both dear and bad. The Country Houses, the Dissenting Academies, and the Scottish Universities did more than Oxford and Cambridge to nourish the widely diffused English culture of that period of our civilisation.

The character, policy and reputation of a College or a University depend mainly upon the dons, and the quality of the dons at Trinity, as elsewhere, was at this time very poor. Mr Winstanley, in his *Unreformed Cambridge*, has estimated the extent and analysed the causes of this long disease of College life. He attributes much of the decadence of the Fellows to their idleness. For the most part they had nothing to do. Very few of them were scholars or researchers; and in the eighteenth century the College administration, the lecturing and the teaching fell into the hands of a small group. The rest, not knowing what to do with their ample leisure, developed uninviting personal eccentricities. They were not subject to the mild discipline of family life, for they were not allowed to retain their Fellowships if they married.[1] Few of them had been brought up as gentlemen, or seen anything outside the world of school and college. Hence the queerness of their manners, which, as Mr Winstanley argues with instance taken from Trinity, were worse than their morals. The morals of some of them have been described by Gunning, let us hope too harshly (*Reminiscences*, II, 113–20).

It is not therefore surprising to find Wordsworth thus writing, in the *Prelude*, of his undergraduate experience (1787–91):

> Nor wanted we rich pastime of this kind
> Found everywhere, but chiefly in the ring
> Of the grave elders, men unscoured, grotesque
> In character, tricked out like aged trees,
> Which through the lapse of their infirmity
> Give ready place to any random seed
> That chooses to be reared upon their trunks.

Whether Wordsworth found any such 'grave elders' in his own College of St John's I am not called upon to enquire, but certainly such 'men unscoured' were to be found in rich plenty on the south side of the wall over which he looked

---

[1] Some indeed kept their wives hidden away in neighbouring towns like Huntingdon. Some were otherwise accommodated.

into Trinity—men like Peck, Backhouse, Thomas Wilson, William Collier, and Thomas Spencer, as Gunning has drawn them.

As we have seen (p. 15 above), the care of the undergraduates had in Tudor and Stuart times been divided up among all or nearly all the Fellows, each of whom acted as Tutor to a few boys or young men, whom he taught and for whose conduct he was personally responsible. In the eighteenth century, partly owing to the almost complete disappearance from the undergraduate body of boys of fourteen and fifteen, the relation of Tutor and pupil had become less close. After 1755 there were only two Tutors in Trinity for the whole College. In the same epoch the College Lecturers and the University Professors ceased to lecture; lecturing was left to the College Tutors, and individual teaching was left to 'private tutors' or 'coaches', external to the College, whose services the undergraduates were fain to hire.

Thus almost the whole official care of the undergraduates in Trinity fell on the two Tutors, helped at the close of the century by two Assistant Tutors. These men were the backbone of the College. Most of the successive Tutors after the middle of the century were good and able men—Whisson, Postlethwaite, Richard Watson, Cranke, and above all Thomas Jones; but some of them had to act with such colleagues as Backhouse or Collier, men of a character unfitted for the care of youth.

The real weakness of the College lay in its control by the Seniority, the eight old men to whom, for no merit but the fact of their survival, the unwise wisdom of the Elizabethan Statutes had committed all power in conjunction with the Master. Not only the present but the future was in their hands, for it was they who chose the new Fellows. In 1786, at least four of the eight Seniors were either notorious for their immoral life or unhinged in intellect. Of the other four, the Vice-Master, Meredith, was the only man of any mark, and he was the most careless of all in the matter of examining the candidates for Fellowships, the issue on which the reformers challenged the Seniority.

The crisis of 1786–7, the successful stand made by ten of the younger Fellows against the Master and Seniors, has always been regarded as the first effective step towards the reform not only of Trinity but of the University as a whole. It coincided with the improved tone in the public affairs of the country in the days of Burke, Wilberforce, and the younger Pitt. Something better was in the air of the new age, and the younger Fellows of Trinity had felt it.

To cut a long story short, 'the Ten'[1] formally complained in a petition to the Master, Hinchliffe, Bishop of Peterborough, that at the Fellowship election of October 1786 some of the Seniority had voted in the election without first examining the candidates.[2] Behind this complaint lay the belief that a worse man had been preferred to a better for reasons of favouritism, though this was not stated in the petition. The Master and Seniors formally censured the petitioners and recorded the censure in the Conclusion Book. The Ten appealed to the Visitor.

Since the epoch of Bentley's trials it had become generally agreed that the Visitor of the College was not the Bishop of Ely but the Crown, at least for every purpose except that of removing the Master. The Crown therefore received the appeal of the Ten, and the Lord Chancellor, Thurlow, dealt with the case. He managed it with tact and ability, and he did substantial justice. He deferred his judgment, and suggested that peace might be restored if the Ten Juniors apologised not for the matter but for the manner of their petition to the Seniority, and if the Seniority expunged the censure on

[1] Their names were Waddington, Baynes, Cautley, Miles Popple, Thomas Jones, Porter, Baskett, Hailstone, Murfitt, and Matthew Wilson.

[2] At that time the method of examination was that each candidate was (or should have been) examined separately by each elector in turn in his rooms, usually in mathematics, philosophy, and the classical languages. The examination of the candidate by the elector could be either *viva voce* or written; it was usually both.

the Juniors from the Conclusion Book.[1] He said outright that all who voted in Fellowship elections ought to examine the candidates. Nominally a drawn battle, it was in reality a victory for the Ten. In the words of Gunning of Christ's (II, 109):

From the date of this memorable appeal, Trinity College assumed that high character in the University which it has ever since maintained. The system of favouritism which had so long prevailed, and by the operation of which so many unfit men had been elected into Fellowships, received its death blow.

Hinchliffe, the Master who had mismanaged this affair, by no means resembled personally the sordid Seniors whose cause he had rashly espoused. He himself was a typical eighteenth-century pluralist and Bishop, a man of culture, dignity and fashion, famous as a preacher with a mellifluous voice, and the splendid presence which our portrait of him recalls. To be at the same time Master of Trinity and Bishop of Peterborough was consonant with the ideas of the times, but led to a considerable neglect of both sets of duties. When Sir Joseph Thomson became Master of Trinity in 1918 he found in a cupboard of the Lodge an enormous ancient key, labelled 'The Palace, Peterborough'. How came it there? The solution of the enigma was not far to seek. Clearly it was the key of the episcopal palace at Peterborough, accidentally left by Hinchliffe in his other house!

Two years after the crisis of 1786–7, Hinchliffe was succeeded in the Mastership by Postlethwaite, who wisely instituted a new system whereby Fellowship candidates sat for a public examination, instead of being privately examined by each elector.[2]

[1] The Ten would not apologise, so the censure remained in the Conclusion Book, where it can still be read, signed by Hinchliffe—*John Peterborough. M.C.*
[2] The best account of the affair of the Ten and the Seniority will be found in Winstanley's *Unreformed Cambridge*, pp. 238–55. See also Gunning, II, 106–20.

While the type of Fellow elected underwent a marked improvement after 1787, the Tutorship of Thomas Jones, one of the Ten, during the next twenty years raised the reputation and thereby increased the numbers of Trinity, so that at the opening of the new century it had fairly taken the lead in the Cambridge world, though the College of Wilberforce and Wordsworth and Palmerston was still a formidable competitor in the undergraduate race for University honours.

Postlethwaite's improved system of examining the candidates for Fellowships is to his credit, and his Mastership (1789-98) coincided with a rise in the fortunes and reputation of the College. This was in part due to the support he gave as Master to the better elements in the College, to Jones as Tutor, and to James Lambert, the ex-Professor of Greek, whom he chose as Bursar, to the indignation of reactionaries and the joy of reformers.[1]

But Postlethwaite had his faults; he was not a thoroughgoing reformer, and I am afraid he is best remembered for his unfortunate collision with the greatest Trinity man of the day, Richard Porson.

Bentley is the king of English classical scholars, but Porson, in the estimation of those able to judge, holds the next place. He had been elected to a Fellowship in 1782, but it was due to run out in 1792 unless he took Holy Orders. This he was conscientiously unwilling to do, and obtained from Postlethwaite a promise of the reversion of one of the two Fellowships tenable by laymen which were in the Master's gift. But Postlethwaite broke his word and gave the lay Fellowship to one of his own relations. He could not understand why Porson refused to take Orders like everyone else. There was an angry scene between the two men, for Porson did not mince his words. It was the collision of two epochs, the easy conscience

---

[1] See Dean Milner's letter to Wilberforce, *Life of Milner*, p. 161, and Gunning, II, 120-1.

and enjoying character of the outgoing eighteenth century, and the more perplexed mind and more earnest character of the coming age.

Since Porson 'had doubts' and also drank,[1] he thought it his duty to remain a layman, though he thereby condemned himself to lifelong poverty and exile from Cambridge. It is true that a few months later (Dec. 1792) Postlethwaite tried to make amends by securing Porson's election to the Professorship of Greek, but as the stipend was only £40 a year, as fixed by Henry VIII when money had a very different value, the great Cambridge scholar was constrained to spend the rest of his life in London to earn a living. He never lectured as Professor (so far at least Porson's conscience was still eighteenth-century!) but he came up from town periodically to examine. As Professor he had rooms and commons in Trinity, and after Postlethwaite's death in 1798 felt more at ease here, and was more frequent in his visits to the College till his own death in 1808. He was buried in the ante-Chapel at the foot of Newton's statue. (*Richard Porson*, by M. L. Clarke, Camb. Univ. Press.)

Porson renewed the Bentleian impress of exact scholarship on Cambridge tradition, but his school became somewhat formalised after his death. His best pupil, Dobree, who became Fellow of Trinity in 1806, ought to have been his successor in the Greek Professorship two years later, but was passed over as too young. When Monk retired from the Professorship in 1823, Dobree succeeded him, but his health had always been bad and he died prematurely in 1825. Dobree was to Porson what Cotes had been to Newton, the true successor—*si quâ fata aspera rumpat.*

---

[1] Another great classical scholar of Trinity, A. E. Housman, the 'Shropshire Lad', once made the following after-dinner speech at a convivial occasion: 'Cambridge has seen many strange things. It has seen Wordsworth drunk, and Porson sober. Here stand I, a better scholar than Wordsworth, and a better poet than Porson, betwixt and between.' An example of Porson's satirical poetry will be found in Gunning's *Reminiscences*, II, 114.

After Porson no English scholar was famous abroad until Jebb two generations later. But reading the Greek classics for pleasure and writing Greek verse with skill were much commoner in England in the nineteenth century than at any other place or time, and commonest of all at Trinity. It may be said that sound classical scholarship lay at the base of much that was best in Victorian literature, certainly in the case of two Trinity men, Macaulay and Tennyson.

The course of improvement was not cut short in our College, as it was elsewhere, by controversy on the French Revolution and by the violent anti-Jacobin reaction that swept over the country in 1792, and continued as long as the Napoleonic Wars. The Trinity dons were divided between Whig and Tory, but not with personal bitterness, and there were no extremists on either side. The College went on minding its own business, little perturbed by the storm.

The touchstone of opinion in the University was the trial of Frend, a Fellow of Jesus who had written a reforming pamphlet on Church and State—some of it foolishly provocative, particularly its remarks on the clergy, but none of it seditious. At that time Dean Milner, the great evangelical Tory, dominated the University from the President's Lodge at Queens'. In 1793 he headed a successful movement to drive Frend out of Cambridge. Frend was put to a sort of trial in the Senate House. Everyone who took the side of justice and commonsense in the matter was marked down as a 'Jacobin', and many were cowed into silence. But Trinity was big enough to shelter open differences of opinion. Thomas Jones, the Tutor, and James Lambert, the Bursar, were not afraid to appear on the floor of the Senate House in the small body of defenders of the accused man, while our Master, Postlethwaite, and his destined successor, Lort Mansel, were active on the other side. The undergraduates in the gallery, including S. T. Coleridge of Frend's own College, with the generosity of youth, demonstrated noisily against the injustice of their elders below.

Frend was driven from the University, but his persecutors were enraged that Trinity should harbour those who had defended him, or tolerate the very mild form of Liberal-Conservatism which Thomas Jones and Lambert represented. Dean Milner aspired to be Master of Trinity with a view to destroying the last asylum of the spirit of political decency and freedom which it pleased him to call 'Jacobinism'. He appealed to his fellow-evangelical Wilberforce to induce Pitt to gratify his ambition. Pitt, however, liked the evangelicals too little, and Wilberforce was not enough of a High Tory to support these designs against the liberty of our College. If Milner had been appointed Master, as he wished, to succeed either Hinchliffe in 1789 or Postlethwaite in 1798, Trinity would have known another Bentleian war of Master against Fellows. Milner was a more honourable and public-spirited man than Bentley, but he was just as self-willed and formidable, and in the joint cause of evangelical religion and authoritarian politics would stick at nothing.

Milner's attack on Trinity in a confidential letter to Wilberforce in 1798 is a tribute to the recent reform of the College:

My idea of Trinity College is this. The management of it is of great academical and even national importance. The foundation and the prospects are so splendid, that it invites and brings students, in spite of the conviction of danger of corrupt principles. The College fills; they have great choice for their Fellows; and in general they choose the most able. Hence it is that either they do now, or soon will, consist of men of talents with few exceptions; and if they get corrupted in their principles, and further if a regard to heterodox and Jacobinical principles be also had, in the election of Fellows, I leave you to judge what sort of a society they may become.

The present Master, so Milner goes on to complain, has not interfered with Jones and Lambert. If Milner had been Master, as he had hoped to be, he would have taken a very different course—so he tells Wilberforce.

'I don't believe Pitt was ever aware', whines the meritorious Milner, 'of how much consequence the expulsion of Frend was. It was the ruin of the Jacobinical party *as a University thing*, so that that party is almost entirely confined to Trinity College.' (*Life of Milner*, pp. 161-3, and see remarks on the letter in *Dict. of Nat. Biog. sub* Milner.)

The choice by the Crown of Lort Mansel to succeed Postlethwaite on his death in 1798 left things much as they were. Mansel indeed was a Tory, and the King wrote to Pitt approving the appointment on the ground that the new Master would 'restore discipline in that great seminary, and a more correct attachment to the Church of England and the British Constitution than the young men educated there have for some time past been supposed to possess'. Two young men from Trinity were at that time specially objectionable to government, Erskine the eloquent defender of accused Liberals in the law courts, and Charles Grey, M.P., who had recently founded 'The Friends of the People', and afterwards, as Prime Minister, secured the passage of the Reform Bill of 1832.

But Mansel was no persecutor or bigot. The most influential friend who had supported his claims to the Mastership had been the liberal-minded Trinity Prince, H.R.H. the Duke of Gloucester, the steadfast enemy of the Slave Trade, who afterwards became Chancellor of the University.[1] The new Master was a man of the world, not devoid of sense and good nature; he wished to live on terms with everyone in the College, including such dreadful 'Jacobins' as Jones, Lambert and Porson. He had previously been known as a sayer of witty things, and a writer of satirical epigrams, some of them not too delicate. He was a good classical scholar and had been Public Orator of the University. He was a man of the old order, round whom the last enchantments of the eighteenth century still lingered, a man of taste, a pluralist, Bishop of Bristol as well as Master of Trinity. He was made Bishop in

---

[1] He was called 'Silly Billy', partly, I think, on account of the unfortunate curve of his large nose, but there were many sillier people among his Majesty's subjects than his nephew William Duke of Gloucester. There is a full-length portrait of him in the Lodge as a Trinity freshman (by Romney), and a Sir Joshua of him in the Hall as a boy in fancy dress.

1808 by the influence of Spencer Perceval, his life-long friend since old Trinity days together. Though Perceval has been called 'our first evangelical Prime Minister', he was not, it appears, above doing an ecclesiastical job for an old friend.

In Mansel's early years as Master, Pitt, though a Pembroke man, was a frequent visitor to Trinity Lodge, where 'Mr Pitt's sofa' was long shown. The portrait of him by Hoppner, now in the drawing-room, was presented to the Lodge the year after his death.

In 1803 Mansel became a widower, and his chief aim in later life was to make the Lodge a pleasant centre of hospitality, whence he could marry off a bevy of pretty daughters who adored their venerable papa. There is an unpublished Life of Mansel, by a relation of his, in the College Library, with interesting illustrations and letters.

Trinity in the eighteenth century contained more noblemen and fellow-commoners than any other College except possibly St John's. The two classes were not clearly distinguishable, for a commoner could put himself down as a nobleman by paying more, and a born nobleman could economise by entering as a fellow-commoner. And this exchange of parts was not unusual. The 'nobleman' wore a hat instead of the academic cap, and his gown had elaborate gold embroidery like that of the Duke of Gloucester in Romney's picture of him in the Lodge. Both noblemen and fellow-commoners dined at the Fellows' table, where they must often have been dreadfully bored. By law or custom they enjoyed in varying degrees exemption from attendance at lectures, exercises and examinations. They were in short invited by the authorities to be idle and to hold themselves apart from their fellow-students; as might be expected, they availed themselves of the first privilege more than of the second. Most of the breaches of discipline in the College could be traced to them, and most of the 'fast' life. But a few of them worked hard, and many of them gained much by residence in a place where learning and intellect were the first considerations, and by contact with the youth of other classes on what were essentially equal terms.

There was in fact much less class distinction at Cambridge than elsewhere in eighteenth-century England. Wordsworth, who was at St John's from 1787 to 1791, thought poorly of the elders, but he wrote of undergraduate society:

> Nor was it least
> Of many benefits, in later years
> Derived from academic institutes
> And rules, that they held something up to view
> Of a Republic, where all stood thus far
> Upon equal ground; that we were brothers all
> In honour, as in one community,
> Scholars and gentlemen; where furthermore,
> Distinction open lay to all who came,
> And wealth and titles were in less esteem
> Than talents, worth and prosperous industry.

When in the nineteenth century the privileges of noblemen and fellow-commoners were one by one abolished, when they competed with everyone else in examinations and in organised games and boat-races, the 'Republic' of undergraduates became even more republican.

The sizar or poor scholar in the eighteenth century was being gradually relieved of menial duties, and was not really a class apart from the ordinary undergraduate or pensioner. Many of the sizars soon became Scholars on the Foundation. A large proportion of the Fellows of the College had once been sizars of Trinity, like Newton himself; the famous Bishop Watson of Llandaff, that lordly and independent man; and early in the following century the great Adam Sedgwick.

Those who had to rely for their chance in life on their 'prosperous industry' in preparing for examinations, naturally worked hard. The ordinary pensioner worked more or less as the case might be, and was much the same kind of person as the 'average undergraduate' of to-day. Hardly anyone came up below the age of seventeen; 'boy undergraduates', like Pitt of Pembroke, were now extremely rare. In the absence of boat-racing and organised games, the usual amusements of the undergraduate, selected according to his inclination and financial means, were pleasure boating on the upper or lower river; fighting the bargees and the town with staves or fists; riding and walking; fishing and shooting. Much less of the land near Cambridge was then drained, wildfowl abounded, and game was very little preserved. Gunning thus recalls his undergraduate days in the seventeen-eighties:

If you started from the corner of Parker's Piece, you came to Cherry Hinton Fen; from thence to Teversham, Quy, Bottisham and Swaffham Fens. In taking this beat, you met with great varieties of wildfowl, bitterns, plovers of every description, ruffs and reeves, and not unfrequently pheasants. If you did not go very near the mansions of the few country gentlemen who resided in the neighbourhood, you met with no interruption. You scarcely ever saw the gamekeeper, but met with a great number of young lads who were on the lookout for sportsmen from the University whose game they carried, and to whom they furnished long poles, to enable them to leap those very wide ditches which intersected the Fens in every direction. (*Reminiscences*, I, 41.)

In the Long Vacation, an engagement as tutor to a gentleman's or nobleman's son often gave the scholar a pleasant change from College to country house, showed him other parts of England and other modes of life, and sometimes opened out to him connections and friendships which in that age of patronage gave a lasting direction to his career. A large proportion of the Bishops and highly beneficed clergy were Oxford and Cambridge men who had been tutors to noblemen's sons.

There was heavy drinking in the eighteenth century both among Fellows and undergraduates; in the words of Gibbon about the dons of his own Oxford College: 'their dull and deep potations excused the brisk intemperance of youth'. But the 'coffee house', where alcoholic liquor could not be obtained, had extended its civilising influence from London to Cambridge. For newspapers, discussion and gossip, the eighteenth-century undergraduates went each to his favourite coffee house, much as in the following century they went to the Union or the Pitt

Club. In 1750 the authorities forbade them to enter a coffee house between nine and twelve in the morning, when they ought to be at their books.

The dinner in Hall at Trinity was at noon in Bentley's day, but by 1799 had been pushed on to half-past two. Both dons and undergraduates dressed for it in knee breeches and stockings. Supper was sent out by the kitchens to a man's own rooms or to those of a friend.

And so passes away the easy-going eighteenth century, with a sound of the drawing of corks. It was the least exalted time in the history of our College, yet even then many had found it the best privilege in life to dwell within its walls, and some had turned that privilege to noble ends.

A NOTE ON NUMBERS

A note on the numbers admitted yearly to Trinity may be interesting as some indication of the prosperity of the College at different periods, and the varying demand on the part of the public for University education, which could then only be obtained in England at Oxford or Cambridge. In one respect the situation remained the same throughout: from the foundation of Trinity onwards to the end of the eighteenth century the Trinity admissions remain about a sixth of those of the whole University. The decadence in the eighteenth century, as far as it is indicated by numbers, is equally marked in Trinity and in the aggregate of the other Colleges. The decline begins before the end of the seventeenth century, and reaches its worst in the decade 1760-9, after which the numbers rise once more, till in the decade 1790-9 the numbers entering Trinity are again what they had been in the palmy days of the Tudors and early Stuarts. After that, the rise is steady and rapid to much greater numbers as the nineteenth century goes on.

In *Admissions to Trinity College*, Rouse Ball and Venn, 1 (1916), 9, 10, Rouse Ball writes:

The number of recorded entries and admissions to the *College* from 19 Dec. 1546 to 31 Dec. 1635, as shown in these volumes, is 4797, showing an average for these 89 years of *about 54 a year*. The number of recorded matriculations in the *University* from the founda-

THE LATER EIGHTEENTH CENTURY

tion of the College (1546) to the end of 1589 is 11,850, and from 1602 to 1635 inclusive is 12,658, showing an average for these 77 years of *about 318 a year*.

From the next three pages (10–12) of the same volume I have made out the following rough figures for the subsequent period, i.e. from the Civil War to the beginning of the nineteenth century. As particular years vary a good deal, I have taken the yearly average for each decade.

Recorded entries and admissions to Trinity:

1640–49 about 49 a year	1730–39 about 24 a year
1650–59 „ 45 „	1740–49 „ 25 „
1660–69 „ 50 „	1750–59 „ 24 „
1670–79 „ 43 „	1760–69 „ 21 „
1680–89 „ 32 „	1770–79 „ 39 „
1690–99 „ 28 „	1780–89 „ 41 „
1700–09 „ 27 „	1790–99 „ 54 „
1710–19 „ 28 „	1800–09 „ 64 „
1720–29 „ 30 „	1810–19 „ 92 „

After that the numbers keep well above 100, rising steadily.

1880–89 about 187 a year
1890–99 „ 191 „
1920–29 „ 226 „

Throughout the eighteenth century St John's had a larger number of yearly entries than Trinity, until the last decade (1790–9) when during the Tutorship of the excellent Thomas Jones (1787–1807) the numbers of Trinity shot ahead.

CHAPTER VIII

THE NEW AGE

Building of the New Court

MASTERS OF TRINITY

1798–1820: LORT MANSEL
1820–1841: CHRISTOPHER WORDSWORTH

LORT MANSEL, as we have seen in the last chapter, was himself imbued with the ideas and standards of the eighteenth century, but during his Mastership the characteristics of nineteenth-century life and thought took form at Trinity, and names appeared in the Lists of the College of men who more than any others gave to it its peculiar ethos in the coming age. Before Mansel died, the more active Fellows included Adam Sedgwick, Monk, Whewell, Julius Hare and Connop Thirlwall, the makers of the new Trinity, and Blomfield who, as Bishop of London, was to help Peel and the Whig Parliamentarians to reform the worst abuses of the Church. There was much in common between all the members of that group. Though some were Whigs and some were Tories in politics, they were all liberal-minded clergymen, ardent educationalists, solid in character and in learning, versed in mathematics and in classical scholarship. Those who were classics first and foremost came from the south; the northerners, Adam Sedgwick and Whewell,[1] were the mathematicians, and were destined to give to the physical sciences their importance in modern Cambridge. But all were men of the twofold learning, classical and mathematical. Their minds were therefore very different from those of their

[1] As a freshman exhibitioner in 1812, Whewell wrote home to his family that he was happy at Cambridge, but pined beside 'the narrow and dirty Cam' for the hills and running streams of the north. Much the same, I expect, was felt in 1804 by Adam Sedgwick as an uncouth sizar from the Yorkshire dale of Dent. He and Byron were among Thomas Jones' last pupils.

contemporaries on the Isis, who were indeed classical scholars, but were soaking the other half of their minds not in mathematics but in patristic theology. And so, ere long, Oxford gave England the Oxford Movement, and Cambridge helped to give her science.

Everyone at Cambridge had to do mathematics; until 1824 there was no other Tripos. But University Prizes and College Fellowships could be won by classical men; Macaulay, who had been 'gulfed' in mathematics, became a Fellow in 1824. In the early years of the nineteenth century the primacy of Trinity lay in classics, as at the beginning of the following century it lay in science. In the list of Wranglers St John's was still a formidable rival, but in the University Prizes and Medals for classics Trinity swept the board. The classical teaching at Trinity was recognised as being very good, and opposition to the establishment of a Classical Tripos arose in part from the fact that some of the smaller Colleges had not the staff to teach Greek and Latin scholarship effectively.

During the first thirty years of the century, the leading Trinity Fellows and undergraduates were deeply interested in English as well as in Greek and Latin literature. The chief subject of discussion among them was the merits of William Wordsworth's poems, which they did much to bring before the world. Strange as it may seem, Whewell wrote sonnets in the Wordsworthian manner, and in 1814 won the Chancellor's Medal for English "Heroic Verse", then a great object of ambition and rivalry in the University, as Thackeray of Trinity has recorded in *Pendennis*. In the twenty years 1814–33 the Medal was won thirteen times by Trinity men; and these winners included—besides Whewell—Macaulay (twice); Praed (twice); Bulwer-Lytton; Christopher Wordsworth, son of the Master and nephew of the poet (twice); and in 1829 Alfred Tennyson was the victor, with a mystical poem only very slightly related to the set subject—*Timbuctoo*![1]

[1] The Cambridge Prize Poems from 1813 to 1858 were published in the latter year by Macmillan. The volume is well worth study by anyone interested in academical or in literary history.

The early history of oratory at the Union is also closely connected with Trinity men—Macaulay and Praed, Bulwer-Lytton and Arthur Hallam, Charles Buller and Frederick Denison Maurice, and Carlyle's friend John Sterling. The last four had also much to do with the early history of the private debating society known as 'the Apostles'.

The mathematical-classical education obtainable at the College at this period produced also a great crop of lawyers. The list of Judges who had been Trinity undergraduates between 1790 and 1820 is very long, and it includes Lord Lyndhurst (Copley) and Lord Chief Baron Pollock, both Smith's Prizemen; and Lord Wensleydale (Parke), fifth Wrangler and Craven Scholar. In a later generation, the College of Bacon and Coke produced two great men, historians of English law, Sir Frederick Pollock and F. W. Maitland himself.

In 1805 Byron came up from Harrow to Trinity. He was, as his Tutor noted, a youth of 'tumultuous passions'. As a nobleman he was scarcely expected to take much interest in the studies of the place, and he did not. He lived 'very fast'. To mention his more innocent pleasures, he was writing his early satires and poems, riding, shooting with pistols and boxing. The weir above Grantchester is called Byron's Pool because he swam there; he also swam matches in the Thames under the training of his friend Jackson, the pugilist, who had more influence upon him than his official Tutor, the excellent Thomas Jones. Byron, observing that there was a statute against keeping dogs in College but none against keeping bears, lodged a bear in the top attic of the tower at the south-east corner of the Great Court, then called 'Mutton-hole corner'.*
He took Bruin for walks on a chain like a dog, and said he 'should sit for a Fellowship', and 'teach the Fellows manners'.[1]

After the poet's heroic death in Greece, a fine statue of

1 *Alma Mater by a Trinity Man*, 1827, has some curious information about Byron's bear and its 'rooms', pp. 165–7. These two anonymous volumes, actually written by J. M. F. Wright who came to Trinity in 1814, contain a good deal of interesting matter, though not all in the best taste.

* [It seems more likely that Byron's bear was kept in the Ram Yard. Byron lived in Nevile's Court, on either D staircase or I staircase. A letter of 26 October 1807 in Moore's *Life of Byron* refers to the bear.]

THE NEW AGE

him was made by the Danish sculptor, Thorvaldsen, and sent to England to a Committee of Byron's friends, who offered it to Westminster Abbey. But the Dean considered that Byron had been too immoral to have a monument in the Abbey. As one of the chief treasures exhibited there was the waxen effigy of Charles II, the decision against Byron's statue may seem singular. But Trinity men can scarcely regret it, for after being hidden away for many years in the vaults of the London Custom House, the statue found in 1843 its perfect home, when at Whewell's suggestion it was placed at the end of the long vista of our Library. There, surely, it is seen to greater advantage and receives greater honour than if it was huddled in a row with half a dozen statues of Victorian statesmen in 'the National Valhalla'.

After the first fall of Napoleon in 1814, the white-haired veteran Blücher was given an honorary degree by the University. He was entertained at Trinity. An immense mob of enthusiasts drew his carriage in by the Great Gate and ran it round the whole circuit of the Court before permitting him to alight at the Master's Lodge. At the feast in his honour in Hall, he was in high barbarian glee, drained the goblet of audit ale, made a spirited speech in German, and on going out under the screens caught up a pretty woman who offered him her hand 'and inflicted several kisses that were distinctly heard at the upper end of the Hall'* (Gunning, II, 292–3). Next year he fought his Waterloo campaign.

In 1820 Lort Mansel died. The new Master was Christopher Wordsworth, younger brother of the poet; like William he had been educated at Hawkshead Grammar School. He was a classical scholar of distinction, who had been many years away from Trinity when he returned as its Master. The portrait of him now on the staircase of the Lodge looks like a surly edition of William. He was a man of sterling qualities, but he was ungracious in manner, and it did not help him in Trinity that he was still loyal to the strictest creed of anti-Jacobin Toryism when a large number of the Fellows were Liberals

* [Another account says that the 'pretty woman' was Mansel's daughter, and the place the Lodge, by a window in full view of the crowd in the Court. (W. Glover, *Memoirs of a Cambridge Chorister* (London 1885), vol. I, p. 158). Gunning does not say that the incident took place 'under the screens', but when the party was 'leaving the Hall' to take coffee with the Master in the Lodge, perhaps by the door on the dais.]

and the tide of time was running fast in the new direction. This led, as we shall see, to quarrels; but first we must record Wordsworth's great contribution to the life of the College, the building of New Court. In this matter at least the new Master was an earnest reformer, for the question of undergraduate discipline appealed strongly to his instinct for order.

There was a great deal being said at that time of the temptation laid in the way of the young men by the fact that most of them had to live in lodgings. It was certainly easier to be 'fast' in lodgings than inside the walls of the College, and the rapid increase in numbers was raising the proportion of those who slept outside the gates. Wordsworth determined that it was the duty of the College to build on a large scale. He made the proposal the moment he became Master. A delay of two years was caused by opposition from the Seniority led by Lambert, formerly regarded as a dangerous 'Jacobin' but now in extreme old age averse to novelty. On Lambert's death, Wordsworth got his scheme through the Seniority, in 1823. Wilkins was the chosen architect.

There had been some thought of building on the site of the Bowling Green, but fortunately this was abandoned in favour of the ground between Bishop's Hostel and the river. This involved moving the College brew-house to its present position nearer the river, and curtailing the space devoted to the Fellows' stables, then an important item in College life. The stables were now confined to the short space between the back of Bishop's Hostel and Garret Hostel Lane.

The area thus obtained was covered by the New Court as it now is. Its great merit was that it comfortably housed so many undergraduates. It is not perhaps the happiest example in Cambridge of the neo-Gothic style of architecture, fashionable in those days when the influence of Sir Walter Scott's romanticism was at its height. Moreover the Fellows were reduced, for reasons of economy, to use stucco for the interior of the Court, where good stone or brick had been originally intended. Even so the enterprise cost £50,000, and both the Master and Fellows acted boldly and generously in carrying through such a plan in the days of severe agricultural depression. A large subscription list, to which George IV contributed £1000, helped out the College finances, but great sums had also to be borrowed.

Trinity thus set an example which other Colleges rapidly followed. Half a dozen years later the new buildings of St John's, on the far side of the river, rose in proud rivalry, presenting, at least towards Trinity, a fairy palace rich in mediaeval fancy. There is a story that Whewell, when Master, objected in his arbitrary manner to people standing on Trinity Bridge. Seeing an undergraduate one day leaning over its northern parapet he accosted him thus: 'Sir, do you know what this bridge was made for?' The answer he expected was 'To go over it', to which Whewell would retort, 'Then, sir, do so'. But the undergraduate happened to be a Johnian, who promptly replied, 'I understand this bridge was erected to give the public the best possible view of the new buildings of St John's'.

Arthur Hallam was an early inmate of the New Court, and in his rooms Alfred Tennyson spent many of the happiest and most formative hours of his life, as described in *In Memoriam*. Among other Trinity friends of the young Tennyson were Edward Fitzgerald, James Spedding and Monckton Milnes.

Christopher Wordsworth had done the College a real service in inducing the Seniority to build the New Court, and he served the University well by initiating a demand for a Classical Tripos to take its place beside the Mathematical; this also attained success in 1822. The fruits of the first years of his Mastership were thus garnered, but after that he seemed to fall out of touch with the life of the place. In the Lodge he was a rather lonely widower without social instinct. In his dealings with the College he was a strict disciplinarian, conscientious to a fault, deficient in the sense of humour and proportion in matters about which he felt strongly. One of these was the frequent irregularity of undergraduate attendance at Chapel, for which he raised the scale of penalties.

Now in those days, when membership of the College was in

effect confined to Anglicans, there could be no theoretical grievance if persons so privileged on account of their religion were expected to attend Chapel. But, in practice, human and undergraduate nature could only brook a moderate amount of this discipline. The Master's own brother William, the great Johnian, had many years before written in his *Prelude* against compulsory Chapel, speaking of

> The witless shepherd who persists to drive
> A flock that thirsts not to a pool disliked.

The *Prelude* was indeed not published till after the poet's death in 1850; one is left wondering whether Christopher ever saw these lines in manuscript, and whether, on William's frequent visits to the Lodge, the brothers discussed a question on which they took such radically opposite views.

Meanwhile the junior members of the College formed in self-defence a 'Society for the Prevention of Cruelty to Undergraduates': they avenged themselves by publishing lists of the attendance of the Fellows at Chapel, which was exposed as setting a very bad example to poor persecuted youth!

The domestic question of compulsory attendance at Chapel became involved in the political question of admission of Dissenters to degrees at the University. After the passing of the Reform Bill of 1832 it was expected that everyone would shortly be so admitted, irrespective of religious creed. There was a great majority for the change in the reformed House of Commons, but the resistance of the House of Lords postponed it for another generation. In the year 1834 many pamphlets and speeches on this controversy were published; and one of the most precious of the Tory arguments was that if Dissenters were admitted to Cambridge, it would be impossible for the Colleges to enforce compulsory Chapel. This enraged that most liberal of divines, Connop Thirlwall, afterwards Bishop of St Davids, but at that time an Assistant Tutor at Trinity. Assistant Tutors were not responsible for discipline; they were the College Lecturers, each attached to a Tutor's *side*: Thirlwall lectured to Whewell's pupils. He somewhat rashly thought it consistent with his office to write a pamphlet not only advocating the admission of Dissenters to Cambridge, but denouncing compulsory Chapel as impious and unprofitable to the religious life.

This was too much for the Master, who dismissed Thirlwall from his Assistant Tutorship, on the ground that an officer of the College had no right publicly to attack its discipline.[1]

The Fellows of the College, especially the Whigs and the younger men, were furious, and even those who, like Whewell, disapproved of Thirlwall's pamphlet, disapproved yet more of the Master's action. Wordsworth found himself more than ever isolated in the College, and wished to retire. But his sense of public duty would not permit him to depart so long as the Whig Ministers remained in power, for they would be certain to advise the Crown to appoint in his place a Liberal, probably Adam Sedgwick. So Wordsworth stayed on, because the Whigs stayed on, year after year, till at last, in the autumn of 1841, a Conservative government came into office, whereupon Wordsworth resigned with comic promptitude, and Peel at once advised the Queen to appoint William Whewell as Master of Trinity.

[1] In the course of the controversy one of Thirlwall's opponents (the Master's son) wrote that 'the alternative was between compulsory religion or no religion at all'; to which Thirlwall replied, 'The difference is too subtle for my grasp'.

The rights and wrongs of the whole affair, in which the Master and Thirlwall were perhaps both to blame, are discussed with customary fullness and impartiality by Mr Winstanley in his *Early Victorian Cambridge*, pp. 73–8, and 388–94. Thirlwall's classical lectures were of first order of excellence, and his influence on undergraduates and popularity with his colleagues made his loss to the College very great indeed (see J. Willis Clark, *Old Friends in Cambridge*, 1900, on him, Whewell, and W. H. Thompson).

CHAPTER IX

TRINITY IN THE VICTORIAN ERA

Renovation of the Lodge Growth of Science
Whewell's Court New Statutes
Cambridge & Trinity Chapel Decoration

MASTERS OF TRINITY

1841–1866: WILLIAM WHEWELL
1866–1886: WILLIAM HEPWORTH THOMPSON

WILLIAM WHEWELL, the son of a master carpenter in Lancaster, was a self-made man. He had the strength of a giant in body[1] and in mind. He did mighty tasks, but in his dealings with men he too often used his strength 'like a giant', so that he was more admired than loved, except by his intimates to whom he showed the affectionate nature which underlay his rough manners. He was magnanimous, and to the College 'bountiful as mines of India', making us the princely gift of the Court called after his name. The statue of him by Woolner in the ante-Chapel gives a good idea of his formidable and rugged power.

He and his friend and fellow-northerner Adam Sedgwick did in their day more than anyone else to promote the new scientific studies in Cambridge, especially at Trinity. Before

---

1 It is a well-authenticated Trinity tradition that Whewell, when Master, jumped up the Hall steps at one leap, a feat that is very seldom accomplished even by youthful athletes. Sir George Young told his son Geoffrey Young that he had actually witnessed this performance; Sir George said that the Master, in cap and gown, found some undergraduates trying in vain to accomplish the feat. He clapped his cap firmly on his head, took the run, and reached the top of the steps at one bound. *

There is a story that a well-known pugilist looking at Whewell said, 'What a bruiser was lost when that man became a parson'.

* [The authenticity of this tradition has been doubted. Whewell was 45 when he became Master, and 62 when Sir George Young came up in 1856. See A. S. F. Gow, *Letters from Cambridge* (London 1945), pp. 221–22.]

he became Master, Whewell had written his *History of the Inductive Sciences*. It was said of him that 'science was his forte, omniscience was his foible'; but surely, rather, the vast extent of his knowledge was his other 'forte'. English and German literature and philosophy, classics, history, architecture, divinity, international law, he knew them all, and much else beside. It was largely through his influence, exerted on Cambridge for many years, that in the fifties the new Triposes were established in the physical and in the moral sciences, and in law. He himself founded the Professorship of International Law. Henry Sidgwick wrote "It is to Whewell more than to any other single man that the revival of philosophy at Cambridge is to be attributed" (Mrs Douglas' *Life of Whewell*, p. 412). It was he who induced the University to choose Prince Albert as Chancellor, partly in the vain hope of avoiding Parliamentary interference with Cambridge through a Statutory Commission, and partly because he knew that the Prince was an educational reformer after his own heart. For Whewell, although in defence of the old College and University Statutes he opposed innovation, made sustained and successful efforts to broaden the scope of academic study. It was no accident that his Mastership was the period when the new Triposes were started; but his death helped to smooth the way for the abolition of religious tests and for other organic changes imposed by Act of Parliament on the University and on the College. Both as academic conservative and as academic reformer Whewell all his life exerted a twofold influence.

From 1824 to 1839 he had been Tutor (side C), but was too much absorbed in his own great studies to pay much attention to his pupils.[1] In October 1841 his connection with Trinity seemed to have reached its end, when he forfeited his Fellowship by marriage. But that very month Peel, in a fortunate hour, called him back to our service as Master.

The first mark that he left on the College in his new capacity was the restoration of the Tudor-Gothic character of the

[1] There is a portrait of him as Tutor, now (1942) in the drawing-room of the Lodge, and on the staircase another of him as Master.

Lodge front. In 1842 he removed from its east face the sash windows which Bentley had inserted (pp. 57–58 above) and replaced them with replicas of Nevile's Elizabethan windows in harmony with the general pattern of the Great Court. But with wise discrimination he left Bentley's windows on the garden side to the west.

As part of this scheme of Gothic restoration, he rebuilt the two bow windows or oriels, one on each side of the Lodge, two storeys high, thus giving much needed light to the depths of the dining-room and the Elizabethan drawing-room above it. The Tudor oriel on the east or Great Court side had been removed in the later eighteenth century (p. 72 above); Whewell rebuilt it, but in a polygonal, not in Nevile's semi-circular, form. Nevile's oriel on the west side of the Lodge had been only one storey high, but a wooden structure had been erected on the top of it to light the drawing-room, probably by Lort Mansel for the benefit of his daughters. (There is a sketch of it by one of those ladies reproduced in the unpublished Life of Mansel in the College Library.) Whewell swept all this away, and built the present oriel through which dining-room and drawing-room look out pleasantly on the Master's garden. Over each of the two oriels he erected a tall narrow gable in the best neo-Gothic style. The carved woodwork in the bow window of the dining-room was put there at the same time; Whewell's arms of three women's heads can be seen upon it.

As the restoration of the Lodge neared completion, a characteristic dispute arose, mildly reminiscent of the fiercer Bentleian controversies on a like subject. The work had been conceived and carried through by Whewell himself, but it was the College that paid for most of it. An old Trinity man, Beresford Hope, had given £1000 towards the restoration of the oriel on the Great Court, and Whewell had given another £250. But the Seniority had readily consented that the rest of the bill for the changes in the Lodge (the whole reached a total of £3765) should be paid by the College. No doubt it was right that the College should pay for repairs in the Lodge on the advent of a new Master (I should be the last to dispute it, after all that was so generously done on that principle a hundred years later!). And when the new Master is a Whewell, the changes will certainly be dictated by him. But the Seniors thought it was going rather far when he put up an inscription in which he claimed to have restored the antique beauty of the Lodge himself, with the help of Beresford Hope, and said nothing about the College which had found two-thirds of the money. The inscription has suffered by a hundred years of weathering, but some of it can still be deciphered round the top of the oriel of the Lodge looking on to the Great Court:

> Munificentia fultus Alex. J. B. Hope Generosi hisce aedibus antiquam speciem restituit W. Whewell Mag. Collegii A.D. MDCCCXLII.*

There was a good deal of aggrieved gossip, and the situation was thus described by one of the youngest Fellows, Tom Taylor, afterwards Editor of *Punch*:

> These are the Seniors who cut up so rough,
> When they saw the inscription or rather the puff,
> Placed by the Master so rude and so gruff,
> Who lived in the house that Hope built.[1]

During the twenty-five years of Whewell's Mastership, Trinity went on from strength to strength. The life of undergraduates and dons was never more vigorous or more varied. The list of Fellows elected during this period included H. A. J. Munro and Jebb in classical scholarship; Clerk Maxwell in physical science; Westlake the international lawyer; Westcott, Lightfoot and Hort who founded that Liberal school of exact biblical scholarship which was as characteristic of Cambridge as the Oxford Movement and its reactions were of the sister University. But the man who was destined to exert perhaps

---

[1] There are various traditional versions of Tom Taylor's lines. Willis and Clark, II, 626–7; Rouse Ball's *Trinity College* (Dent, 1906), pp. 12–13. The suggestion in Mrs Stair Douglas' *Life of Whewell*, p. 252, that the restoration of the Lodge cost only £1435. 4s. 6d. is not correct.

* [The inscription was removed when the stonework of the oriel was repaired in 1965.]

the greatest moral and personal influence on Cambridge in the last forty years of the century was the philosopher Henry Sidgwick; when he was elected to a Fellowship in 1859, he was the centre of a group of young Trinity men whose friendship for one another the passing years never dimmed—Henry Jackson, the Yorkshire Platonist who was to mean so much in the social life of later Victorian Trinity; Edward Bowen, the author of the Harrow Songs, the most original and eccentric of schoolmasters; and my father George Otto Trevelyan, whose *Horace at Athens* (1861) and *The Cambridge Dionysia* enjoyed for fifty years a wide popularity as representing the intellectual high spirits of classically educated young men of Trinity in that golden age.

It has been said with some measure of truth that mountaineering in Switzerland was begun as an English habit in the middle of the century by young Cambridge dons. Of these the chief was Leslie Stephen of Trinity Hall, but there were many Trinity alpinists also in that early period, above all Sir George Young. Roof-climbing at Cambridge came in a later generation, in the time of Sir George's son, Geoffrey Young, author of the *Roof-climber's Guide to Trinity* in the last years of the century.

Rowing, as we know it, was fully developed in Whewell's time, with bumping races on the lower river and all the glorious life of First and Third Trinity.[1] The growth of organised games led in 1861 to the leasing by the College of land from St John's to form the Trinity Cricket Field; this ground was purchased in 1901 and is now our Old Playing Field in the angle between Grange Road and Adams Road.

The plan of admitting undergraduates to reside during a part of the Long Vacation was adopted by the College at Whewell's suggestion. At the same time the 'reading party' in the Lakes, Wales, Scotland or Ireland was a favourite way of using and enjoying the late summer, the party reading hard

[1] The Trinity Boat Club dates from 1825. For its history see W. Rouse Ball's *History of the First Trinity Boat Club*, Bowes and Bowes, 1908. It contains also much information about Third Trinity and the shadowy Second.

all morning and walking hard all afternoon. Such reading parties had been known in the days of the Regency (*Alma Mater*, II, 58). But the love of hill scenery and hill-walking so characteristic of the Victorians, and the facilities of railway travel, made this custom more and more general as the century went on. Sometimes a 'coach' took his pupils; sometimes undergraduate friends, reading perhaps different subjects, formed a party for themselves.

Whewell was twice married, very happily. His marriages and his income made him a rich man, and he devoted his wealth to our advantage. His gifts and bequests to the College in connection with Whewell's Court were of the value of £100,000. He had the foresight to buy up the land opposite the Great Gate, and he found the money to build on it the two new Courts that together bear his name. Part of the room rents he left to maintain the Whewell Professorship of International Law,[1] part to found scholarships for the University and the College.

It was unfortunate that Whewell's Court was built in the worst period of Victorian architecture. Alterations made recently to the windows have improved it to some extent, but it is still gloomy. Nevertheless the service to the College of a hundred sets of rooms is immense, and though the two new Courts may be as ugly as other Cambridge buildings of that period, Whewell's promptitude, in obtaining the site on which they now stand, saved Trinity from being obliged in later years to spoil the Backs by building there, so that even from the point of view of amenity we must be grateful to his generosity and his foresight.

One very beautiful thing we owe to Whewell—the avenue of elms which he planted in 1843 at his own expense in the Fellows' garden or Roundabout; he placed them in a line

[1] A famous Trinity man, Sir William Vernon Harcourt, the future Liberal statesman, was the first Whewell Professor in 1869. Harcourt has left his mark on the present Old Guest Room in Nevile's Court, in the form of his family arms and motto, the flamboyant peacocks and 'Vernon semper viret', on the stucco of the ceiling.

with the limes on the other side of the Backs road, which were already at that time 170 years old. Whewell's elms are now at their prime, while the ancient limes are sadly decayed, and are being one by one replaced.* The site of the Fellows' garden had been leased by the College from the University in 1803, and was purchased after Whewell's death for £4000 (Willis and Clark, II, 647).[1]

Whewell died in 1866 and was succeeded by W. H. Thompson, formerly Tutor and Regius Professor of Greek. During the twenty years of his Mastership great changes took place in the character of the society owing to Parliamentary legislation which altered the Statutes of the University and of the College. These reforms, based on the reports of a series of Royal Commissions, had begun to affect the College in Whewell's later years, but had not then gone very far, partly because of his resistance. But Thompson and the society over which he presided (1866–1886) were more ready than their predecessors to accept and even to promote changes long overdue. Trinity men were now in the forefront of the reform movement in Cambridge, no longer deprecating but welcoming the help of Parliament to remove from the living academic body the shackles of an age out-worn. In 1868 thirty-two out of the sixty Fellows, including four out of the eight Seniors, signed a petition in favour of the removal of religious tests.[2] Especially strong was the sympathy aroused in the College by the disinterested act of Henry Sidgwick; in 1869 he resigned his Fellowship, because the declaration of religious orthodoxy,

[1] There is an accurate and detailed picture of life at Trinity in 1840–5 in *Five Years at an English University* by C. A. Bristed, an American who was a Scholar of the College, and on his return to the United States wrote this book to explain English Universities to his countrymen (Putnam, New York, 1852). In J. W. Clark's *Old Friends at Cambridge and Elsewhere* (Macmillan, 1900) there are good articles on Whewell, Thirlwall, and W. H. Thompson. Mr Winstanley's *Early Victorian Cambridge* is invaluable for the history of the period.

[2] *University Tests. An Apology for their Assailants*, by Sir George Young (Macmillan, 1868).

* [The lime avenue on the west side of the river was completely replanted in 1949.]

which he had been able sincerely to make ten years before as a condition of his election, had since then ceased to represent his belief. The scrupulosity of this renunciation, which neither law nor public opinion demanded, was eminently characteristic of Sidgwick.

Two years later the Test Act of 1871 applied the remedy, and opened the University and the Colleges, with their offices and endowments, to all persons irrespective of creed. This great change was soon followed by others, until finally the College Statutes of 1882 entirely superseded those of Elizabeth's reign. By the new constitution thus acquired by Trinity, essentially unaltered to this day, the rule of the Master and eight Seniors was replaced by the power of a Council consisting partly of the College Officers and partly of representatives chosen by the general body of the Fellows including the youngest; the College Meeting of all the Fellows was henceforth the final seat of authority. The power of the Seniors as such disappeared, and that of the Master was greatly reduced.[1]

During this period of rapid reform, the double obligation on the Fellows to take Holy Orders and to refrain from marriage was completely abolished. As a consequence of these and other changes, the last thirty years of the century saw the growth of a new Cambridge and a new Trinity. The undergraduates, except that they were no longer all of them nominally members of the Church of England, were perhaps not very different from their predecessors, though they were rather more often in friendly touch with their elders. But the Fellows ceased to be a society of celibate clergy and became a society wherein laymen greatly predominated and in which there was an increasing proportion of married men.

Scientific studies and the scientific point of view were also on the increase. In this movement, which affected the whole

[1] W. H. Thompson, the Master, favoured these changes; but he uttered at a College Meeting an epigram characteristic of the dry wit for which he was famous, directed in a kindly spirit at the reforming zeal of a group of junior Fellows: 'We are none of us infallible, not even the youngest of us.'*

* [Thompson's remark was provoked by a proposal for revising the Statutes made by Gerald Balfour, one of the youngest Fellows, at the College Meeting of 30 March 1878, and was greeted by 'a shout of uncontrollable laughter'. Balfour was the brother of A. J. and F. M. Balfour; his motion was, incidentally, seconded by Coutts Trotter, perhaps the weightiest of the Seniors.]

University, our College played a leading part. The first Professor of Physiology (1883) was Sir Michael Foster, whom Trinity had made the first Praelector in that subject a dozen years before. The first Cavendish Professor of Experimental Physics was Clerk Maxwell. Indeed from its foundation in 1871 to the present day the Cavendish Professorship has always been held by a Trinity man: Lord Rayleigh succeeded Clerk Maxwell, J. J. Thomson succeeded Rayleigh, Rutherford succeeded J. J. Thomson, and Sir Lawrence Bragg has succeeded Lord Rutherford.*

Other brilliant scientific Fellows of Trinity elected in the seventies were George Darwin, J. N. Langley, William Kingdon Clifford and Francis Maitland Balfour; the last named, a naturalist of the highest promise, had his career cut short at the age of thirty-one by a climbing accident in the Alps; the affection with which he was regarded in the College is commemorated in the bust of him on the Library staircase below the portrait of his brother Arthur, the Prime Minister, a man scarcely more charming or more gifted than the younger brother whom he survived by almost half a century.[1]†

But during the period of W. H. Thompson's Mastership, the College was equally productive in subjects other than physical science. Frederick Pollock and Frederick Maitland were both Trinity men of that time, destined together to create a new science and philosophy of the history of English Law. And in Classics, though Jebb left Cambridge for Glasgow in 1875, there were young men like S. H. Butcher and Walter Leaf, while the presence of Verrall in our midst was a perpetual stimulus and challenge and joy.

It was during this period of academic reform and vigorous intellectual life that the College began to fulfil a duty too long neglected at Cambridge, in providing lectures in all sorts

[1] The Trinity Prime Ministers number six: Perceval, Grey, Melbourne, Balfour, Campbell-Bannerman and Baldwin. St John's can claim Goderich, Aberdeen and Palmerston, and another statesman greater than most Prime Ministers—Wilberforce.

* [Sir Lawrence Bragg's successor as Cavendish Professor was not a Trinity man. Arthur Cayley ought probably to be added to Trevelyan's list.]

† [The bust of F. M. Balfour is now in the Reading Room.]

of subjects, outside the routine lectures delivered by Tutors and Assistant Tutors to the *sides*. The College also now began to give systematic personal instruction and supervision by means of Fellows on the College Staff, instead of leaving the undergraduate to pay a private 'coach' to prepare him for the University examination.

The educational policy of Trinity in the last half of the nineteenth century was vigorous and liberal, endowing many fields of teaching and research. In this period Trinity held a real primacy in Cambridge, which she could not claim during the eighteenth century when St John's was her rival on equal terms. Nor in the twentieth century is the primacy of our College so clear as it was, not because our own level has fallen, but because the level of other Colleges has risen, largely owing to the improvement of secondary education in the country as a whole.

Moreover the University itself, during the last seventy years, has gradually resumed functions of lecturing and research which it had long ago abandoned to the Colleges. One of the greatest of academic reforms has been the taxation of the Colleges (the richer at a higher rate) for the benefit of the University. The large sums which Trinity pays annually, together with the similar contributions of other Colleges and the help of the State, now enable the University to perform functions which in the last century were either not performed at all or were left to the initiative of the Colleges, not least our own. Moreover, the vast growth of physical science with its laboratories and its endowments has greatly increased the importance of the University as such, diverting wealth and functions that under the old system would have gone to the Colleges. The Colleges as such are relatively less important than they were eighty years ago. Trinity men have not jealously opposed this trend towards a larger unity. Our motto has been 'Cambridge first'.

These remarks have carried me far ahead of the years of W. H. Thompson's Mastership (1866–86), when such changes were only in their initial stage.

During that period the interior of the College Chapel acquired its present appearance. We have seen that the woodwork of the stalls, the organ loft and the baldachino are of the period of Bentley (p. 60). But the painting on the roof and on the wall space above the stalls, and the stained-glass figures in the windows, are characteristic Victorian products of the years 1871–5. They were elaborated on a scheme of religious and historical allegory devised by no less authorities than Westcott and Hort.*

In the ante-Chapel, Roubiliac's statue of Newton had stood alone in its glory for a hundred years, until in Whewell's day the statues of Bacon and Barrow were set to flank it on either side.† In Thompson's time Woolner's statues of Macaulay and Whewell were added. Jebb's inscription under Macaulay's statue, one of the best of the many specimens of elegant Latinity on the memorials in the ante-Chapel, contains the appropriate words

Qui primus annales ita scripsit ut vera fictis libentius legerentur.

The statue itself has merit, but my father used to say to me that it misrepresented his uncle in one particular: it shows him sitting sideways, whereas he always sat straight forward and never with legs crossed.‡

In Montagu Butler's Mastership the last of the statues in the ante-Chapel was erected to commemorate our great poet. The curious can detect the bowl of Tennyson's beloved clay pipe peeping out from under the laurel wreaths on the bas-relief below. It was put there by a secret conspiracy between the sculptor Thornycroft and the donor Harry Yates Thompson, a life-long friend of Montagu Butler, who was well aware of the Master's old-fashioned dislike of the nasty habit of smoking! Did Butler notice it? He never said anything.

* [The windows remain in the Chapel, but were removed from the Ante-Chapel after the Second World War. The paintings on the walls and ceiling of the Chapel, which had deteriorated badly, were painted over in 1962. The nineteenth century decorations are described in detail in Willis & Clark *Architectural History of the University of Cambridge* (Cambridge 1886), vol. II, pp. 588–600.]

† [Newton's statue now stands on its own at the west end; the others were moved to their present positions 1948–49.]

‡ [An engraving of Macaulay in his Library at Holly Lodge also shows him sitting with legs crossed.]

CHAPTER X

MONTAGU BUTLER 1886-1918

IN THE late fifties, young men at Trinity, especially the brilliant group of whom Henry Sidgwick was the centre, looked up to Montagu Butler with a very special regard and affection, as to an elder brother. From early youth he seemed destined some day to be Master. But when W. H. Thompson died in 1886, Butler had been away from Cambridge for a quarter of a century, as Head Master of Harrow, in succession to another Trinity man, C. J. Vaughan; Vaughan had restored the reputation and scholarship of the School, which Montagu Butler maintained, while its fame was further enhanced by a third Trinity man, Edward Bowen, the writer of its songs. During Butler's long absence at Harrow great changes had taken place at Cambridge, to which I have referred (pp. 102-3 above). Jim Butler in his Memoir of the Trinity life of his father[1] thus summarises the old regime:

Even the Statutes of 1860-1, in the framing of which he himself had taken an active part, left the administration in the hands of the Master, who must be in the Orders of the Church of England, and the eight Senior Fellows, all of whom must be unmarried. All Fellows had to be members of the Church of England, and unless they held certain offices were bound to take Orders within seven years from their M.A. degree. Fellowships were tenable for life, but with few exceptions were vacated on marriage, or institution to a benefice of a defined value; in compensation, however, the Fellows who contemplated marriage might count on receiving the offer of a College living.

---

[1] *Henry Montagu Butler, Master of Trinity College*, 1886-1918, by J. R. M. Butler, Longmans, 1925. The photographs in that volume give a better idea of the unique blend of dignity and loving-kindness of which Butler had the secret than the Herkomer portrait of him in the Lodge, or the caricature of him by Orpen in the Hall.*
* [The portrait in the Lodge is a copy of Herkomer's.]

By 1886 all this had been swept away. The body of Fellows was becoming every year a more and more lay society; not a few of them at that time regarded clergymen with a certain degree of suspicion, the aftermath of the recent struggle which had emancipated the College from clerical control, and science from the trammels of the Book of Genesis. Moreover the younger Fellows were now, first and foremost, specialists, since they had of recent years been chosen by the test of learned Dissertations, instead of by examination as in Whewell's time. The literary, classical, and liberally religious atmosphere of the Trinity in which Butler had been reared was giving place to a different ethos, though the older tradition still had, and I hope will always retain, a large influence on the many-sided culture of the College.

Butler, therefore, was coming back to a place that he loved and idealised, but very imperfectly knew. Moreover, under the Statutes of 1882, the Master no longer ruled; henceforth he was only to reign. Could Butler cheerfully submit to these limitations after his long and successful autocracy at Harrow? The marvel is that he did so to perfection, and ended his thirty years of Mastership more venerated and beloved by Trinity men, past and present, near and far, than any of his predecessors, unless haply Nevile.

But when Lord Salisbury appointed him in 1886, doubts were felt, even among his old friends, as to his adaptability to the changed conditions. It was even said that the appointment of a schoolmaster was 'a snub given to academic work'. The lay party, flushed with their recent victory, had hoped that a layman would be Master, as the new Statutes allowed. If the choice had lain with the Fellows, they would not improbably have elected Sidgwick or Rayleigh.

It is to the credit of all concerned that these clouds gradually dispersed. Butler, indeed, for all his mild manners, had strong views, and he often had to accept decisions which pained and even shocked him. But such was his benevolence of soul that no quarrels arose, and if there was ever unkindness it was not on the Master's side. I will refer to one of these disputes in which he yielded sorrowfully but with a good grace, because it concerns the buildings of the College.

It had long been apparent that more space was required to house modern books in the Library, if it was to be of much use in the future to members of the College, especially to undergraduates.[1] Since no one would dream of touching Wren's masterpiece, it was clear that new buildings must be erected somewhere in its neighbourhood. In 1887 Butler inspired a Committee of the Council to report in favour of a scheme on which he had set his heart.

The proposal was to erect a new two-storeyed building north of, and parallel to, the north side of Nevile's Court, making use of the ground then occupied by the Master's kitchen garden, stables and coach-house.... The new building was to be in the style of Wren; it was to be of red brick, with a frontage of Portland stone facing the river, and it was to be connected with Wren's building by a 'not unsightly stone bridge'. The ground floor was to be used for books, the upper storey to provide 'a gallery for portraits of distinguished members of the College, and for other art purposes, including room for books bearing upon art'.[2]

This would cost at least £35,000, of which it was suggested that £11,000 should come from College Funds. For the rest, Butler was confident that he could successfully appeal to the generosity of old Trinity men, as he had appealed to old Harrovians for the cost of his great building operations at Harrow. He was further encouraged by remembering how Barrow, taking the bull by the horns, had .begun Wren's library regardless of expense (pp. 44-5 above).

But he was doomed to severe disappointment. The Council, after long debates, turned down his scheme in favour of a

[1] Undergraduates in those days had more books of their own than they often have now. The development of College and departmental libraries and reading-rooms for their benefit is a growth of the last half-century.

[2] J. R. M. Butler's Memoir, pp. 47-8.

much less ambitious 'Library Annexe' that still serves our purposes to-day. That long, low outcrop of red brick is cramped up against the back of the northern side of Nevile's Court, as if trying to escape notice. It is indeed just as well that it is hidden away and that its external appearance is familiar only to the inhabitants of the Lodge; its interior usefully supplies the needed book-stacks and the reading-room for undergraduates.

The Council had rejected Butler's more daring plan on financial grounds: it was a time of agricultural depression, and the College then possessed few sources of external income other than rent and tithe. But the grounds on which posterity may be inclined to be grateful for the decision are aesthetic. What, we may wonder, would it have been like, this second large library 'in the style of Wren' joined to the old one by 'a not unsightly stone bridge', if it had been built in 1890 in the fat red brick of the period, by the architect, Sir Arthur Blomfield, who actually built in its stead the Library Annexe?*

In 1892–3 Blomfield rebuilt the west wing of the Lodge somewhat in the same style and in the same material. It looks out over the Master's garden from its south-east corner, replacing some older and less extensive offices and rooms. It is the one utilitarian part of the whole ancient and beautiful house. Every new Master and his wife have reason to be grateful to the College for adding the convenience of modern kitchens and a row of modern bedrooms; the latter were originally the 'nursery wing' where Montagu Butler's second family was reared.

From 1893 to 1897 the Council and the general body of the Fellows were in constant discussion of another building scheme, the erection of a hundred more sets of undergraduate rooms in the paddocks, on either side of the far end of the lime avenue. The proposal, though very nearly carried, was abandoned, largely because the opinion of old Trinity men, when consulted, appeared hostile to building on the Backs.

Since then no notable addition has been made to the College buildings,† but much care and money have been spent on the

* [Blomfield was also the architect of the 'new' Bishop's Hostel, completed in 1878.]
† [See pp. 116 and 117.]

maintenance of our architectural heritage. Every year in peace time a portion of one of the Courts is repaired during the Long Vacation.

An important change in the use of certain College buildings remains, however, to be noticed. After the last War and the death of Montagu Butler, the College in 1920 took away from the Master's Lodge its south end abutting on the Hall, and converted it into a Parlour below and a Combination Room above, for the use of the Fellows. They were thus enabled to give up the 'Old' Combination Room (as it is now called) with its portraits of eighteenth-century noblemen and magnates on the walls, for purposes of concerts, meetings and semi-official occasions of all sorts, while the room that had been the Parlour became the present Junior Combination Room for undergraduates. The new accommodation for the Fellows on the north side of the Hall is much more convenient. The rooms taken from the Lodge were panelled and fitted up for this purpose at the expense of Howard Morley and other old Trinity men. The Combination Room where the Fellows now drink their port formerly contained the Master's study and his bedroom.[1] A College room in the north-west angle of the Great Court was given in exchange to the Lodge, and was fitted up with bookshelves as the Master's study: the first to occupy it as such was J. J. Thomson.

I shall make no attempt to describe the intellectual and social life of the College during the last fifty years. It is too large and many-sided a theme to be dealt with here. But I will mention one or two of the men who were playing leading parts in my undergraduate days at the close of the last century, besides J. J. Thomson and the men of science. William Cunningham was an imposing figure as he passed slowly across the Court in the shadow of his great archdeacon's

[1] The south end of the Combination Room, next the Hall, used to be the Master's bedroom. It was there that Whewell, in his last moments, had the curtains drawn back so that his dying eyes could rest on the Great Court, the place he loved best on earth.

hat, looking like some high personage of Trollope's Barchester; but his capacious mind was evolving the new science of Economic History as an academic study, which has since grown to such great proportions. The History School of Cambridge, then in its most critical period of rapid growth, found its true centre in a set of rooms in Nevile's Court; there, amid his strange foreign books, sat Lord Acton, with a brow and beard like Plato, ready all day long to welcome any visitor seeking historical knowledge, whether it was Maitland or the humblest undergraduate.

Meanwhile Sir James Frazer of the *Golden Bough*, modest, shy and friendly, was doing his life's work here as a Research Fellow. The chief among the intellectual influences of the College at that time were Henry Sidgwick,[1] Verrall, and McTaggart, the Hegelian, not to mention younger philosophers who are still alive, but whose influence even then was beginning to be felt. Henry Jackson was the social centre of the older men; while his friend St John Parry, the Senior Dean, gathered to his famous 'Sunday evenings' undergraduates of the most various sorts and sets. It was the period of those memorable 'rags' organised by the 'Magpie and Stump' and inspired by the wit of Carr Bosanquet, of which the 'Gordon Riots' was the most famous. Such was Trinity when I first knew it, some fifty years ago.

A. E. Housman, the 'Shropshire Lad', equally distinguished as Latin scholar and English poet, spent the last twenty-five years of his life (1911–36) very contentedly as a Fellow of Trinity. He was notoriously not easy to please, but he let himself be pleased in our society. It might have been expected that the severity of his thought and temper would have refused to melt in the beams of Montagu Butler's expansive benevolence and voluble optimism. But it proved otherwise. Housman recognised the Master's unique quality, and in the inscription he composed for the commemorative brass in the ante-Chapel

[1] Sidgwick at this time resided in Newnham College, where his wife was Principal. They both did great things for Newnham and for the general position of women's education at Cambridge in its early days.

he showed not only his own skill in Latin but a nice appreciation of Butler's rare qualities:

> VIRI INTEGRI, SANCTI, IUCUNDISSIMI.
> FUERUNT IN ILLO MULTAE LITTERAE,
> ANTIQUITATIS MAGNA NOTITIA,
> MEMORIA TENACISSIMA,
> FACILIS ORATIONIS ELEGANTIA,
> CUM GRAVITATE IUNCTUS FACETIARUM LEPOS.
> IDEM COLLEGII SUI AMANTISSIMUS,
> ANIMI NON IN SUOS TANTUM BENIGNISSIMI,
> CARITATEM QUA CETEROS COMPLEXUS EST
> SIBI CONCILIAVIT.
> NATUS A.D. VI NON. IUL. A.S. MDCCCXXXIII
> CHRISTI IN FIDE,
> QUAM SERMONE, ELOQUENTIA, VITA
> COMMENDAVERAT,
> OBDORMIVIT A.D. XIX KAL. FEB.
> A.S. MDCCCCXVIII

EPILOGUE

IN the original Epilogue to this book Trevelyan wrote: 'It is not my intention to say anything of the life of the College in the twentieth century. Its recent history is involved with the lives of many who are still with us, and it is too near us to be seen in perspective.' Thirty years on, however, it seems clear that he had accurately discerned the pattern of development which has determined the history of Trinity in the twentieth century.[1] The continuing tendency of the reforms of this period—some of them the result of recommendations of the Royal Commission of 1919, of which Trevelyan was a member, many of them the result of changes made since he wrote—has been to diminish further the importance of the Colleges in relation to the University, and the predominance of Trinity among the Colleges.

Nevertheless the two or three decades immediately before the First World War have as strong a claim as any to be described as a golden age of College life, and the generations of men who came up then include names as famous as almost any in its history. A. N. Whitehead, Bertrand Russell, G. E. Moore, G. M. Trevelyan, Ralph Vaughan Williams, G. H. Hardy, J. H. Jeans, A. S. Eddington, J. J. Thomson, F. G. Hopkins, A. E. Housman, C. D. Broad, D. H. Robertson, E. Rutherford, W. H. Bragg, W. L. Bragg, R. H. Fowler, F. W. Aston, to mention only the celebrated dead,[2] earned international reputations which lent great lustre to the College, and acted as a magnetic force to attract to it gifted men from all over the world. It was an age, too, when the social and intellectual lives of the undergraduates, their clubs and societies, centred on the College more than ever before.

The war of 1914–18 interrupted all this. Like the rest of

[1] See p. 105.
[2] The list includes eleven members of the Order of Merit, seven Nobel Prizemen, and four Presidents of the Royal Society. G. I. Taylor, O.M., must now (1976) be added to this list.

their generation Trinity men flocked to join the colours, and normal undergraduate life almost came to an end. A military hospital was, for a time, set up in the cloisters of Nevile's Court, and the New Court was occupied by officer cadets. For a time also the life of the Society was marred by unhappy divisions which culminated in the dismissal in 1916 of Bertrand Russell from his College Lectureship by the College Council after he had been convicted of an offence under the Defence of the Realm Act committed in the course of his activities as a pacifist.[1]

In 1918 Sir J. J. Thomson was appointed to succeed Montagu Butler as Master, and was succeeded as Cavendish Professor by Rutherford, who returned to Cambridge as a Fellow of Trinity. At the end of the war the breach with Russell was soon healed and the tensions the episode had produced in the Society disappeared. The College was thronged with undergraduates as never before and men straight from school mingled with veterans of the trenches.[2] But 600 members of the College had died in the war, and their names were inscribed on the panels at the east end of the Chapel. The life of the College resumed much of its pre-war pattern, though signs of change were becoming more apparent. The new Statutes of 1926, which resulted from the recommendations of the Royal Commission of 1919, made changes which were important in the domestic life of the College. The Mastership ceased to be a life appointment. The tenure of junior Fellowships became conditional upon research, and life tenure of Fellowships became in general the reward for long service rather than a privilege acquired with first election.

College lectures came to an end and were replaced by lectures organised centrally by Faculties for members of all the Colleges.

[1] See G. H. Hardy, *Bertrand Russell and Trinity College* (with introduction by C. D. Broad). Cambridge 1970.
[2] Prince Albert, later King George VI, and his brother Prince Henry, Duke of Gloucester, were in residence as undergraduates 1919–20; his grandson, the present Prince of Wales, was in residence 1967–70. King Edward VII was in residence as Prince of Wales in 1861.

To some extent this formalised what was already happening; but it also signified the trend away from a life centred on the Colleges. The same tendency was apparent in the growth of the number of research students, which increased after the institution of the Ph.D. degree in 1919. The teaching of research students, at any rate in Science, could not be organised except on a University basis; but the College continued and indeed increased the amount of help it gave in providing financial support for research students at a time when provision of grants from public funds was not as general as it has since become.

J. J. Thomson, who had presided over the College with homely dignity and modesty, interesting himself in every aspect of its life, died in office in 1940. G. M. Trevelyan was appointed to succeed him, the first Master to be appointed with a fixed retiring age. During the Second World War a more discriminating policy in the use of trained man-power meant that the College was not so completely denuded of undergraduates as it had been in the earlier war. The *Letters from Cambridge*,[1] through which Mr A. S. F. Gow kept his pupils on active service in touch with the College, provide a vivid picture of College life during the War. Through talks and speeches, and most notably through this book itself, Trevelyan made the College more conscious of its past than anyone else had done, at a time when the future looked very dark indeed.

The Second World War took a smaller toll of dead than the First but there were 400 names to record on the memorial on the west wall of the ante-chapel. Once again the post-war world saw the College crowded—indeed overcrowded—with undergraduates. One of the most urgent problems to be faced after 1945 was the need for more rooms and there have been few years in the last twenty-five in which new buildings were neither being erected nor planned. The first was the hostel in Green Street completed in 1948. New rooms were also acquired in Trinity Street and more men fitted into College sets especially in the New Court. In 1959–61 Angel Court was built between Trinity Street and the Great Court. Since then more renovation has gone on in Trinity Street and Sidney Street and new

[1] London, 1945.

EPILOGUE

hostels have been converted from large houses in Bridge Street and Grange Road. The Wolfson Building, south of Whewell's Courts, completed in 1972, represents the largest single new building put up since Whewell's Courts, but there are plans and space for further extensions beyond the Fellows' Garden, should they be found necessary.[1] At the same time the College has undertaken a programme of renovation and restoration unparalleled in its history. Between the wars useful and necessary work was done, especially in the internal reorganisation of the Great Court and of the Junior Combination Room, rebuilt by Sir Edward Maufe. But these achievements have been overshadowed by a programme which included redecoration of the Chapel and of the Hall, construction of a new Kitchen and reconstruction of the old, provision of running water and central heating in most College rooms and most recently, the first major overhaul of the Wren Library since it was built, which goes far to restore its pristine appearance both within and without.

Trevelyan retired in 1951 and was succeeded by Lord Adrian. Two developments which have had considerable effect on the life of the College were already apparent, but they have since become much more dominant influences. One is the increase in the number of Fellows, and the other the increase in the number of members of the College doing research and other post-graduate work.[2] Both reflect very closely two of the main ways in which all Colleges have changed in the latest decades. At the same time the College has adhered closely to a policy of not increasing significantly the number of those admitted as undergraduates.

The increase in the number of Fellows is partly due to a desire to cover more subjects in College teaching, and partly to a policy designed to reduce the number of University teachers who do not also hold College Fellowships. It is partly also the

[1] Two hostels for seventy persons were begun in 1976.
[2] In 1913 there were 64 Fellows and some 75 postgraduate students; in 1938 the numbers were 70 and 79 respectively; in 1951, 90 and 126; in 1965, 110 and 135; in 1971, 117 and 193. The office of Tutor for Advanced Students, with responsibility for men who come from outside Cambridge to do post-graduate work, was created in 1960.

result of the generous provision for life Fellowships made in 1926: men who elsewhere would have been compelled to retire from their Fellowships at the age of 65 or 67, have here remained Fellows in the full sense of the word. The result is that the Society is not only larger than that of any other College but also one in which the span of age and experience is wider. At present there are no fewer than nine Fellows who were first elected before 1918, all of them comfortably over the age of 80.[1]

Lord Adrian, the first Master of the College to be elevated to a lay peerage, retired in 1965;[2] like Trevelyan before him he had by the unanimous and enthusiastic wish of the Fellows been prolonged in office to the latest age, 75, allowed by the Statutes. He was succeeded by Lord Butler, the first Master to come from outside the College since 1700, but one who has close family ties with Trinity and the happy precedent before him as a migrant from Pembroke College of Thomas Nevile. Happy and appropriate, because his Mastership, like Nevile's, may also in retrospect be characterised by great building activity. It has already been marked by other important changes. The tutorial system has been considerably altered. The number of Tutors has been increased and a new admissions system has been adopted. Partly in response to trends in society at large and in universities generally there has been considerable relaxation of rules deemed appropriate to the college system in the past.[3] It is too early to establish the importance of these changes in the life of the College, but the perspective of more than six hundred years of its history and pre-history may give some guidance.

1 Four have died since 1972, two after reaching the Age of 90. The Senior Fellow in 1976, J. E. Littlewood, elected in 1908, is also a nonagenarian.
2 In 1967 Lord Adrian became the first resident Chancellor of the University since John Fisher was elected in 1504. He resigned the office in 1975.
3 In 1974 the statutes were altered to make possible the admission of women as members of the College.

INDEX

Acton, Lord, 112
Adrian, Lord, Master, 40 note, 117, 118
Addison, Joseph, 60
Albert, Prince, 97
All Saints' Church, 7
Angel Court, 116
Anne, Queen, 61-2
Arrowsmith, John, Master, 34
Aston, F. W., 114

Babington, Humphry, 36, 43
Backhouse, James, tutor, 75
'Backs', the, *see* Walks, etc.
Bacon, Francis, 30, 73
Balfour, Arthur, Lord, Premier, 104
Balfour, Francis Maitland, 104
Balfour, Gerald, 103 note
Barrow, Isaac, Master, 16, 38-47, 56, 106, 109
Beaumont, Robert, Master, 13, 18
Bentley, Miss Joanna ('Jug'), 65
Bentley, Mrs, 65
Bentley, Richard, Master, 16, 25-6, 41, 48, 50-68, 98, 106
Bill, William, Master, 13, 17-18
Bishop's Hostel, 45-6, 92
Blomfield, Sir Arthur, architect (1829-99), 110
Blomfield, Charles, Bishop, 88
Blücher, visit of, 91
Boats, the, 100 and note
Bosanquet, Robert Carr, 112
Bowen, Edward, 100, 107
Bowling Green, the Fellows', 6, 52, 55, 92
Bragg, Sir Lawrence, Professor, 104, 114
Bragg, Sir William, 114
Brewhouse, the, 92
Bridge, the, 35 and note
Broad, C. D., 40 note, 114, 115 note
Brooke, Samuel, Master, 33
Buller, Charles, 90
Bulwer-Lytton, 89-90
Butcher, S. H., 104
Butler, Lord, Master, 118
Butler, Montagu, Master, 42 note, 106-13, 115

Buttetourte, Roger, his house, 3-4, 8
Byrom, John, 65
Byron, Lord, 90-1

Caius, Gonville and, 4
Cambridge Platonists, 37
Cartwright, Thomas, 18
Cecil, William, Lord Burghley, 15
Cecils, the, at St John's, 30
Chancellor's Medal, 89
Chapel, the (and ante-Chapel), 7, 18-20, 31-2, 56, 59-60, 66, 106, 115; attendance at, 93-5
Charles I, 40; statue of, as Prince, 27
Charles II, 39-40, 42, 47, 73, 91
Chaucer, 5
Christ Church, Oxford, 10, 51-2
Christopherson, John, Master, 13, 17-18
Clerk, Maxwell, Professor, 104
Clifford, Prof. W. K., 104
Clock Tower, the, or Edward III Gateway, 6-7, 19, 23, 60-1
Cloisters, *see* Nevile's Court
Coffee-houses, 85-6
Coke, Sir Edward, 27, 30
Colbatch, John, 56, 62
Coleridge, Samuel Taylor, 80
Collier, William, tutor, 75
Comber, Thomas, Master, 33, 37
Combination Rooms, old and new 55-6, 72, 111
Comedy Room, 1 note, 29-30, 32-3 note
Conyers Middleton, 56, 62
Cotes, Roger, 54-6, 60, 71 note
Council of the College (1882), 17, 103, 115
Cowley, Abraham, 31 note 6
Cromwell, Oliver, 34-6
Croyland, Robert de, his house, 3, 6
Cunningham, William, Archdeacon, 111-12

Dame Nichol's Hythe, 1 note
Darwin, George, 104
Dobree, Peter, 79

INDEX

Dogs in College, 48–9
Downing College, 43
Dowsing, William, 35–6
Dryden, John, 31, 50

Eddington, A. S., 114
Edward, II, 3–4
Edward III, 3–4; statue of, 23
Edward III Gateway, *see* Clock Tower
Edward IV, 6
Edward VI, 16
Edward VII, 115 note
Elizabeth, Queen, 14–16, 18–19, 24, 28, 30, 49
Ely, Bishops of: Moore, John, 51, 61–3; Fleetwood, William, 63; Green, Thomas, 63–4
Emmanuel College, 35
Erskine, Thomas, Lord, 82
Essex, Earl of, 30
Essex, James, architect, 69–70, 72–3
Eton, 5

Fellowships, conditions of tenure, 16, 36–8, 74, 78, 102–3, 107–8, 115; methods of election, 75–7, 108, *see also* 'Mandates' and 'pre-elections'
Ferne, Henry, Master, 34, 39–40
Fisher, John, 8, 118
Fitzgerald, Edward, 93
Foster, Prof. Sir Michael, 104
Fountain, the, 14, 24, 26
Fowler, R. H., 114
Franciscans or Grey Friars, Cambridge, 13–14, 20, 26
Frazer, Sir James, 112
Frend, William, 80–1

George I, 61, 63 note
George II, 61
George III, 73, 82
George IV, 93
George VI, 115 note
Gibbon, Edward, 85
Gloucester, Henry, Duke of, 115 note
Gloucester, William, Duke of, 82–3
Gow, A. S. F., 96 note, 116
Great Court, 12, 14, 21–6, 48, 69, 72–3, 91, 98; 'Mutton hole corner', 90, 117

Great Gate, the, 3, 7, 26, 54–5, 61, 91
Grey, Charles, Reform Premier, 82
Grinling Gibbons, 44
Gwyn, Nell, 42

Hacket, John, Bishop, 21, 45
Hacket, John, Vice-Master, 63–4
Halifax, Charles Montagu, Earl of, 41, 50
Hall, the, 24–6, 42, 61, 86
Hallam, Arthur, 90, 93
Harcourt, Sir William Vernon, 101 note
Hardy, G. H., 41 note, 114, 115 note
Hare, Julius, 88
Harrow School, 90, 100, 107–9
Henry, VI, 5–6
Henry VIII, 7–14, 17, 21, 36, 79; picture of, 42 and note; statue of, 26–7
Herbert, George, 31, 50
Hervey de Stanton, 3, 7
Hill, Thomas, Master, 34
Hinchliffe, John, Bishop and Master, 69, 72, 76–7
Hobson, carrier, 14, 25
Hooper, Dr Francis, 35
Hope, Beresford, 98–9
Hopkins, F. G., 114
Hort, Fenton, 99, 106
Housman, A. E., 50–1 note, 79 note, 112–13, 114

Jackson, Henry, Vice-Master, 100, 112
'Jacobinism' of Trinity, 80–2
James I, 27, 49
Jeans, J. H., 114
Jebb, Sir Richard, 52 note, 80, 99, 104, 106
Jeffreys, George, Judge, 50
Jesus College, 47, 80
Jones, Thomas, tutor, 75, 78, 80–2, 87, 88 note, 90

Ken, Bishop, 42
Kidman, robber, 72
King's Childers Lane, 1, 7, 29, 33
King's College, 5, 10, 36
King's Hall, 3–14, 19, 21
Kitchens, the, 24–5, 72–3, 117

INDEX

Lady Margaret, 8, *see also* St John's
Lambert, Prof. James, 78, 80–2, 92
Langley, J. N., 104
Laud, Archbishop, 31
Leaf, Walter, 104
Library, Nevile's, 23–4; new (Wren's), 24, 43–5, 48, 70–1, 73, 91, 117; Annexe, 109–10
Lightfoot, Bishop, 99
Lodge, *see* Master's Lodge
Loggan's Prints, 48 and *passim*
Lort, Mansel, Bishop and Master, 49, 69, 82–3, 88, 91, 98
Lyndhurst, Lord, 90

Macaulay, Thomas Babington, Lord, 50, 53 note, 56 and note, 80, 89–90, 106
Maule, Sir Edward, 117
McTaggart, Ellis, 112
Magpie and Stump', 112
Maitland, F. W., 90, 104, 112
'Mandates' and 'pre-elections', 46–8
Mansel, *see* Lort Mansel
Marvell, Andrew, 31 note, 32
Mary Tudor, Queen, 14–18, 19–20
Mary II, Queen, 51, 83
Master's Lodge, 16, 19, 23, 28–9, 54 note, 57–9, 62, 65–8, 72–3, 83, 98–9, 110–11; oriels of, 25, 57, 72–3, 98–9; Judges and, 27 and note, 29, 57; Master's garden, 1 note, 55, 98, 109–10
Maurice, Frederick Denison, 90
Mawe, Leonard, Master, 33
Meredith, Moore, Vice-Master, 75–6
Michaelhouse, 3–4, 7–8, 10–13, 24
Mill Street, 1, 8 note
Milner, Dean, President of Queens', 80–2
Milnes, Richard Monckton, Lord Houghton, 93
Milton, John, 24 note, 25, 36
Minchin, Robert, carpenter, 45–6
Monk, James, tutor, later Bishop, 52–4, 79, 88
Montagu, Charles, *see* Halifax
Montagu, Hon. John, Master, 39, 48, 51
Moore, G. E., 114
Morley, Howard, 111

Munro, H. A. J., 99

Nevile, Thomas, Master, 6–7, 21–32, 69, 118
Nevile's Court or Cloisters, 21, 24–5, 43–5, 69–70, 112, 115
Nevile's Gate, 27–8
New Court, the, 92–3, 115
Newton, Sir Isaac (1642–1727), 15 note, 38–42, 46–7, 54–6, 60–1, 66, 71, 73, 106
Noblemen and Fellow-Commoners, 15, 71–2, 83–5
North, Hon. John, Master, 44–5, 47–8

Observatory, the, 54–5

Palmerston, Lord, 78, 104 note
Parker, Matthew, Archbishop, 9–10
Parr, Queen Katharine, 10
Parry, St John, Vice-Master, 112
Pearson, John Master, 39–40
Peck, Samuel, 75
Peel, Sir Robert, 88, 95, 97
Pembroke College, 21, 83, 118
Pensioners, 4 and note, 12, 14–15
Perceval, Spencer, 83
Physwick's Hostel, 8 note, 12
Pitt, William, 81–4
Plate, the College 34–5, 71–2; the Nevile Cup, 25
Playing Fields, 100
Pollock, Sir Frederick, 90, 104
Porson, Richard (1759–1808), 52 note, 79–70, 82
Postlethwaite, Thomas, Master, 69, 77–82
Praed, Mackworth, 89–90
Prime Ministers, Trinity, 104 note

Queen's Gate, the, 24, 29 note, 61, 69

Ray, John, 38, 70
Rayleigh, 3rd Baron, Professor, 104, 108
Redman, John, Master, 10, 14, 17
Richardson, John, Master, 33
Robertson, D. H., 114
Rokeby, Justice, 27
'Rostrum' in Nevile's Court, 45–6
Roubiliac, sculptor, 38, 60, 70–1, 106
Royal Society, the, 38, 40

121

INDEX

Russell, Bertrand, Lord, 114, 115
Rutherford, Ernest, Lord, 104, 114, 115

St John's College, 3, 8, 14, 30, 52, 71, 73–4, 78, 83, 87, 89, 93, 100, 104 note, 105
St Michael's Church, 7
Scaliger, portrait of, 66
Sclater, Sir Thomas, 36–7, 43
Sedgwick, Prof. Adam, 50, 88, 95
Seniority, the, 17, 25, 53, 58–9, 75–7, 92, 103, 107
Sherman, John, 37
Sidgwick, Henry, 38, 97, 100, 102–3, 107–8, 112
Sidney Sussex, 13, 26, 34
Sizars, 15 note, 84
Smith, Robert, Master, 54–6, 69–71
Somerset, Charles Seymour, 6th Duke of, 61
Spanheim, Ezekiel, 66
Spedding, James, 93
Sports, undergraduate, 24–5, 48 note, 85, 90. *See also* Boats and Playing Fields
Stanton, *see* Hervey de Stanton
Statutes of the College, 16–17, 48 note, 53, 62, 102–3, 107–8, 115
Stephen, Leslie, 100
Sterling, John, 90
Still, John, Master, 13, 16, 21
Taylor, Tom, 99
Tennis Court, the College, 24
Tennyson, Alfred, Lord, 46, 71, 80, 89, 93, 106
'The Ten', protest of, 76–7
Thirlwall, Connop, later Bishop, 88, 94–5
Thompson, Harry Yates, 106
Thompson, W. H., Master, 28, 96, 102–7
Thomson, Sir Joseph John, Master, 77, 104, 111, 114–15, 116
Thornhill, Sir James, 42, 65–6
Thorneycroft, sculptor, 106
Thorvaldsen, sculptor, 91
Trevelyan, George Macaulay, Master, 41 note, 114, 116, 117, 118
Trevelyan, Sir George Otto, 100, 106
Trotter, Coutts, 103 note
Tutors and tutorial system, 14–15, 75, 78, 94–5, 105, 118

Undergraduates, age of, 30–1, 75; numbers of, 73, 86–7
Vacation, the Long, 85, 94–5, 100–1, 111
Vaughan, C. J., 107
Verrall, A. W., 104, 112
Visitors of the College, 61–4, 76–7
Wales, Charles, Prince of, 115 note
Walker, Richard, Vice-Master, 64–66
Walks, 'Backs', gardens, etc., 46, 101–2, 110, *see also* Master's garden *under* Master's Lodge
War of 1914–18, 73, 14, 115
War of 1939–45, 116
Watson, Richard, Bishop, 75, 84
Wensleydale, Lord, 90
Westcott, Bishop, 99, 106
Westlake, Prof. John, 99
Westminster, Scholars, 49–50
Whewell, William, Master, 25, 37, 73, 88, 99–102, 106, 111 note
Whewell's Court, 101
Whisson, Stephen, tutor, 75
Whitehead, A. N., 114
Whitgift, John, Master and later Archbishop, 13, 15, 18, 24 note, 28–30
Wilberforce, William, 78, 81, 104 note
Wilkins, John, Master, 34, 38–40
Wilkins, William, architect, 92
William III, 41, 51
Williams, R. Vaughan, 114
Willughby, Francis, 38, 70
Winstanley, D., Vice-Master, on eighteenth-century dons, 74
Winthrop, John, 31
Wolfson Building, 117
Woolner, sculptor, 71, 106
Wordsworth, Christopher, Master, 88, 91–5; his son, Christopher, 95 note
Wordsworth, William, of St John's, 61, 71, 74, 78, 79 note, 84, 89, 91, 94
Wren, Sir Christopher, 43–6

Young, Geoffrey Winthrop, 96 note, 100
Young, Sir George, 96 note, 100